Anyone who finds themselves striving for rest and unsure of how to practically attain it will be guided by *All Who Are Weary*. This book edifies and encourages believers to lay down burdens they were never intended to carry, and to take up the gracious yoke of Christ. Packed with biblical backing and practical wisdom, this book helps illuminate the path of ministry so many of us walk.

AMY GANNETT, author, Bible teacher, and founder of Tiny Theologians

One thing every human being will experience, if not yet then eventually, is the pain of weariness. In this hopeful, empathetic, gospel-saturated book, Sarah does a great job helping the reader navigate wearying realities including worthlessness, worry, comparison, and a vague sense that our lives don't matter. Along the way, she puts forth the gospel as the solution at every turn. If you or someone you know are feeling less than uplifted and are struggling to find joy, I highly recommend that you read this book.

SCOTT SAULS, senior pastor of Christ Presbyterian Church and author of *Beautiful People Don't Just Happen: How God Redeems Regret, Hurt, and Fear in the Making of Better Humans*

In *All Who Are Weary*, Sarah Hauser marks a life-giving path toward rest. It's not the way of shallow self-care but the abundant life offered in Jesus Christ. If you are wearied by ordinary days, exhausted by extraordinary suffering, or just tired of your self-focused life, you can linger over the deep and ancient truths of this book—and find renewed hope.

JEN POLLOCK MICHEL, award-winning author and speaker

All Who Are Weary moved me to tears more than once. I not only saw myself in Sarah's stories, I saw myself in the Bible's story. I saw Christ lifting my burdens, my grief, my insecurities, and offering me a much lighter load. I saw the gentleness of the God who has walked with me through years of chronic pain, heartbreak, and loss. This book reminded me why the heart of God—a heart full of compassion for His weary children—is never old news to sinners and sufferers like me.

QUINA ARAGON, author of children's books *Love Made, Love Gave,* and *Love Can*

Authentic and raw, *All Who Are Weary* is balm to the anxious soul. Sarah Hauser does a marvelous job weaving her personal story with rich theological truths that will steady and strengthen the worn-out soul. Winsome and wise, I'm thankful for this book.

LAURA WIFLER, author, podcaster, and cofounder of Risen Motherhood

Equal parts encouraging and applicable, I finished *All Who Are Weary* with a deep exhale, softened shoulders, and unclenched fists. Combining vulnerable stories of grief and depression with rich, biblical insight—Sarah gently guides readers to see how true rest is available to all of us, no matter our circumstances. A compassionate, much-needed reminder that just because we live in a broken world, doesn't mean we have to limp our way through it.

ASHLEE GADD, founder of Coffee + Crumbs and author of *Create Anyway: The Joy of Pursuing Creativity in the Margins of Motherhood*

As I read *All Who Are Weary*, my tired soul breathed a sigh of relief. Sarah Hauser is an eloquent storyteller who shows us how Jesus' life, death, and resurrection is the hope we need when all hope feels lost. To the one who worries, or who seeks perfection, or who constantly compares, or who feels like they are drowning in despair—this book is for you.

MICHELLE AMI REYES, award-winning author of *Becoming All Things*

Steeped in honesty and tenderness, Sarah's words remind us that the God of all things is near, even in the darkest depths of our stories. This book whispers into our hearts that even at our most weary, God cares for us with compassion and mercy, allowing us to release what was never ours to hold.

KAYLA CRAIG, author of *To Light Their Way* and *Every Season Sacred* and creator of Liturgies for Parents on Instagram

Tender and truthful, *All Who Are Weary* offers readers a hope-filled approach to trusting the Lord with the lives we have been given—even if they aren't what we expected. I am so thankful for Sarah's honesty and compassion in writing a beautiful, Christ-centered resource for everyone who feels weighed down by the burdens of life. Highly recommended.

ANN SWINDELL, author of *The Path to Peace* and owner of Writing with Grace

If there is a book that makes a person feel less alone in the world, this is it. Drawing from her own experience, Sarah expertly explores topics that are universal to all of us—grief, sadness, loneliness, comparison, despair, worthiness—and serves as a guide as we wind our way through these complicated and deep narratives and emotions. She helps us find our way home—to God, to ourselves, and to one another.

KRISTA GILBERT, author of *Reclaiming Home*, coach, cohost of *The Open Door Sisterhood Podcast*

Friend, the book you hold in your hands is a gift—and an invitation. Sharing honest stories of her own suffering, exploring the testimonies of Christians from Augustine to Esau McCaulley, and digging again and again into Scripture, Sarah tells the truth about the burdens we carry and points us back to the gentleness of God, whose burdens are always light.

CATHERINE MCNIEL, author of *Fearing Bravely*, *All Shall Be Well*, and *Long Days of Small Things*

ALL WHO ARE WEARY

SARAH J.
HAUSER

———

MOODY PUBLISHERS
CHICAGO

FINDING TRUE REST
BY LETTING GO
OF THE BURDENS
YOU WERE NEVER
MEANT TO CARRY

Edited by Amanda Cleary Eastep
Interior design: Ragont Design
Cover design: Erik M. Peterson
Cover illustration of people with blocks © 2021 by RLT_Images / iStock (1322010096).
All rights reserved.

ISBN: 978-0-8024-2941-4

Originally delivered by fleets of horse-drawn wagons, the affordable paperbacks from D. L. Moody's publishing house resourced the church and served everyday people. Now, after more than 125 years of publishing and ministry, Moody Publishers' mission remains the same—even if our delivery systems have changed a bit. For more information on other books (and resources) created from a biblical perspective, go to www .moodypublishers.com or write to:

Moody Publishers
820 N. LaSalle Boulevard
Chicago, IL 60610

1 3 5 7 9 10 8 6 4 2

Printed in the United States of America

For Colson

And for Dad

I have much to be thankful for.

CONTENTS

AUTHOR'S NOTE

WHEN TALKING ABOUT GETTING the help we need, especially during hard seasons, my friend Katie reminded me that no one builds a house with just one tool. I don't need to be a contractor to know she's right. No house—and no life—is built with only a hammer.

In these pages, I share some of my own struggle with depression and an experience with suicidal ideation, as well as stories from others who have walked through their own challenges. But this book is not a replacement for the guidance of professionals who can speak specifically into your life. I share pieces of what I've learned in my own counseling sessions, but I am not a counselor or a therapist—and this book isn't intended to replace one. I also talk about my decision to begin medication for depression, but my story is not intended to be a substitute for advice from a trusted medical professional.

I wholeheartedly believe God, in His grace, has given us a variety of tools to help us let go of what is wearing us out and holding us back from experiencing the rest we have through Christ. I offer my words— my stories and my study of Scripture—as one tool among many. I pray the Holy Spirit will help you hold on to what's helpful and discern what your next steps might be.

INTRODUCTION

SO MANY OF US are exhausted—but not just physically.

We're worn down deep in our souls, bearing a heaviness we can't seem to shake. We feel like we're never doing enough. We question every decision, worry incessantly, or burn ourselves out because we refuse to ask for help.

We carry so much, and the weight is crushing us.

The exhaustion shows up when you lie in bed at night, staring at the ceiling, replaying the scenes of the day, wishing you'd done a thousand things differently. It's a deep fatigue that appears when you're finally alone in the car and find yourself crying for no discernible reason. It's a tiredness that comes from feeling like a failure, agonizing over the future, or constantly trying to keep up with someone else's expectations. It's emotional and spiritual burnout that manifests itself in neck tension or insomnia or ulcers or other physical symptoms.

But what if we didn't have to feel so soul-weary?

What if, even when life is hard, we didn't have to feel overloaded by our burdens? What if, even when our tears weigh heavy, our souls could be light?

It's hard to believe that kind of peace, that deep rest, is even possible. During a particularly dark season, my counselor told me she believed I wouldn't always feel as despairing and discouraged as I was then. I didn't believe her. Besides, I knew even if I got through that season, another hard one would be waiting for me. *How could I ever get through this—and still have the strength to handle whatever inevitably comes next?*

It turns out, she was right—not because circumstances changed, but because God changed me.

My mom used to write down Scripture verses and quotes on index cards. She'd keep them everywhere—the bathroom, her purse, the car cupholder. She'd memorize the verses and remind herself of truths as she quoted Christian authors she'd read.

After she passed away, my family divided up those cards. There must have been hundreds, and now above my desk I have a stack of three-by-fives with my mom's elegant cursive. On one card, she wrote a line about Corrie ten Boom. Corrie was a Dutch Christian who, with her family, hid Jews in their home during World War II. She was arrested and eventually brought to the Ravensbruck concentration camp. *The Hiding Place* recounts her story, and in it she wrote, "Life in Ravensbruck took place on two separate levels, mutually impossible. One, the observable, external life, grew every day more horrible. The other, the life we lived with God, grew daily better, truth upon truth, glory upon glory."[1]

Reading the words of Corrie's story written out by my mom on that index card moved me to tears. The thought that someone could live through the atrocities of the Holocaust and still experience a life with God that grew better and better . . . it's hard to believe.

But I want that kind of faith, don't you?

My mom passed away from pancreatic cancer, and for the two years before her death, I watched her outward life get harder. I saw her body deteriorate. But I also witnessed an inward life that daily grew better because of a good, generous, and all-sufficient God.

Paul wrote in 2 Corinthians, "So we do not lose heart. Though our outer self is wasting away, our inner self is being renewed day by day" (2 Cor. 4:16). This book is about finding renewal for our inner selves. It's about giving up what's burning us out and pursuing joy and endurance instead. It's a book for all who are weary and weighed down, those who are tired to their core. It's for those who want to find a deep rest for their soul that can never be taken away—no matter what happens.

Your outer self may be wasting away. Your outward life may feel like it's falling apart. Your circumstances may be complicated or just mind-numbingly ordinary. But even so, your inner life can be formed into something stronger, more radiant, more secure than ever before.

You can feel at rest in your soul even while your body breaks down. You can know peace even in chaos. You can throw off the soul-crushing burdens of worthlessness, condemnation, worry, self-sufficiency, insecurity, comparison, perfectionism, insignificance, and despair— because you were never meant to carry those things in the first place. And because of the life, death, and resurrection of Jesus, you can take up the easy yoke and light burden He offers instead.

I wrote this book out of my own wrestling, my own depression and grief and tears. And I write as someone still growing in these truths. I struggle at times to throw off the weights Satan keeps trying to heap on my back. But I have also tasted the sweetness of knowing there's no condemnation for those in Christ. I've known the goodness of a God who cares for me. I've found hope knowing that what we see now is not the end of the story.

I've seen—in my own life and in the lives of others—that rest doesn't depend on our circumstances. It depends on our God.

And He's here, with open arms, offering deep soul rest to us all.

Chapter 1

FINDING REST FOR YOUR SOUL

"Come to me, all who labor and are heavy laden, and I will give you rest. Take my yoke upon you, and learn from me, for I am gentle and lowly in heart, and you will find rest for your souls. For my yoke is easy, and my burden is light."

    • Matthew 11:28–30

What crooked paths I trod! What dangers threatened my soul when it rashly hoped that by abandoning you it would find something better! Whichever way it turned, on front or back or sides, it lay on a bed that was hard, for in you alone the soul can rest.

    • St. Augustine

I SAT IN MY CAR in the Panera Bread parking lot with my phone held against my ear talking to my counselor. My twins were at preschool for a couple hours, while my youngest munched on Cheerios in his car seat behind me. This setup became my regular rhythm that winter—phone appointments when I had to keep only child number three content.[1]

A heaviness weighed me down, but I didn't know why. I'd been back in weekly counseling sessions for a few months. I felt stuck, as if I was treading water. I wasn't sure if I could ever stop treading and constantly feared I'd be asked to hold a brick. Even the smallest shift in our schedule, added responsibility, or interpersonal tension felt like that brick. I couldn't keep kicking my legs, and many days left me gasping for air. *What was wrong with me?*

On the outside, life seemed pretty good—three healthy kids, a warm home, family and friends who loved me. But on the inside, I was smothered by condemnation, worry, and despair. I felt lost and sad for a thousand reasons that seemed both completely ridiculous and utterly debilitating at the same time.

I tried to explain all this to my counselor, attempting to put my confusion and weariness into words. I felt like a terrible mother, insecure in my work, inadequate as a wife, joyless in everything. Motherhood and marriage are no cakewalk, sure, but these were gifts I asked for, gifts I prayed for. I had even prayed to have twins, and God said yes. *Why couldn't I escape this darkness when from the outside, my life looked pretty near perfect?*

"It's like there's a dark, windowless room," she said. "You used to be outside the room. But there's a battle going on for your mind, and every time you believe a lie, it's as if you've opened the door to that room a little further." As she spoke, I started to see how with every lie, I took one more step inside, until eventually the door slammed shut behind me—and there I was, unable to escape a darkness so heavy, so all-encompassing, I'd forgotten life outside even existed.

"Now, you're at the point where you need someone—God, counseling, your husband, friends—from outside to unlock the door and pull you out."

My eyes watered as I prayed that no one parked close enough to witness me ugly cry. I could barely string a couple words together. Instead, I nodded my head and mumbled, "That's it. That's exactly it."

I had been letting go of the truth and taking one shaky step after another toward the darkness. When I yelled at my kids, I would think, *You're a terrible mom.* When an article I wrote got rejected, I believed, *Your writing is pointless.* When I saw someone else doing all the things I thought I should be doing, all the "more important" things, all the things I thought made a "real" difference in the world, I too easily fell for the lie that said, *You're worthless.*

I'd been trapped in this dark, windowless room, and my attempts to fix the issue over the past year had been no more freeing than if I'd been rearranging furniture. At times it got more comfortable, but I was still in the room.

My call ended, and I rummaged through the car to find a napkin or tissue to wipe my mascara-streaked face. I drove home exhausted but sensing that there may be hope from this cycle of self-condemnation, this joyless living. The door to the metaphorical room seemed to be cracking open. I knew it wouldn't be a quick and easy journey out, but for the first time in years, I felt a lightness to my soul.

WORN AND WEARY

You might know what it's like to walk around with your shoulders sagging, your head down, and your eyes only half open.[2] Maybe sleep deprivation is to blame. Maybe it's stressors at work, health concerns, life with a newborn, or the weariness that comes from sitting awake waiting for our teenager to come home.

But our exhaustion can run much deeper. Many of us are worn emotionally, spiritually, mentally. We're burned out by the pressure to perform; we're tired of fear grabbing us by the ankles; we wish we could stop constantly feeling like we're letting people down. A solid night of sleep or a weeklong vacation would help. But that only scratches the surface.

We need deep rest for our souls. We need to step out of the darkness, to let go of the burdens we were never meant to carry. We need to abandon the lies, fears, and unhealthy expectations. Only then can we carry what we *are* meant to carry with joy and endurance. Only then can we confidently step forward into what God *has* called us to do.

Our culture so often preaches a message telling us to do whatever makes us happy. But Christ has so much more for us. He calls us to not just build a life for our own gain. Rather, *He calls us to build for the kingdom of God.* We're given the task of loving God and loving others, of living lives that reflect His character and His kingdom. That's a weighty and good responsibility. It's work worth doing, a burden worth carrying.

But we will never be able to do that well if instead we're carrying a whole bunch of junk that trips us up and wears us out.

COME TO ME

In Matthew 11, Jesus preaches to the crowds gathered around Him. He speaks of giving rest to the weary, saying, "'Come to me, all who labor and are heavy laden, and I will give you rest. Take my yoke upon you, and learn from me, for I am gentle and lowly in heart, and you will find rest for your souls. For my yoke is easy, and my burden is light'" (Matt. 11:28–30).

At first glance, His words sound like a quick fix or a magic spell we can utter to feel energized and less stressed out. Or these verses become cliché, a phrase used as a pick-me-up, void of the real meaning and depth they carry.

Jesus doesn't offer pithy sayings or shallow optimism. *He offers Himself.* He offers deep relief that we cannot find anywhere else. He tells us that true rest is found when we take up the yoke of Christ, coming to Him instead of forging our own path.

Jesus doesn't slap a fresh coat of paint on a tired and tattered world. He remakes us. He offers a different way of living that doesn't hide our pain or sorrow. It doesn't gloss over our scars or even our failures. He offers the only way that is *good* and that allows us to live with joy and endurance, come what may.

Before Jesus gives His invitation for listeners to come to Him, He has choice words for others in the crowd. He denounces the cities where He's done the most miracles. He proclaims "woes" on the people who didn't repent. He says scary stuff to the people rejecting the truth of who He is and the kingdom He's building: "Woe to you, Chorazin! Woe to you, Bethsaida! For if the mighty works done in you had been done in Tyre and Sidon, they would have repented long ago in sackcloth and ashes. But I tell you, it will be more bearable on the day of judgment for Tyre and Sidon than for you" (Matt. 11:20–22).

Yikes. No wonder some people hate Him. He's just pronounced judgment on the places where He's shown up in the greatest ways. Yet the people in these cities rejected Him—and Jesus rebukes them for it. They, of all people, should know better. They should have recognized the Son of God when they saw all He'd done so far.

But then, Jesus goes on to say this:

> "I thank you, Father, Lord of heaven and earth, that you have hidden these things from the wise and understanding and revealed them to little children; yes, Father, for such was your gracious will. All things have been handed over to me by my Father, and no one knows the Son except the Father, and no one knows the Father except the Son and anyone to whom the Son chooses to reveal him." (Matt. 11:25–27)

Do you hear the contrast between these two scenes? The "woes" are spoken to those who rejected Jesus, those who should have believed. They saw His miracles; they saw all He was doing—yet they chose to go their own way. But then Jesus thanks the Father for those who have heard. He says "little children" here, meaning those who are humble and acknowledge their dependence on God.[3]

The Jewish leaders would have been considered "the wise." They were the learned who thought they had God's approval and supposedly knew all about the Messiah. In those days, Jewish tradition said that obtaining wisdom involved learning the law and all its finer points. You needed to be a scholar. For the average Jew that was like being a rocket scientist. It was unattainable.

But here, Jesus says, *No. It's not the so-called wise who will understand what God is doing. It's the humble; it's those who know they don't have it all together. Those who know Me are the ones who know the Father.*

For the original listeners, this would have been scandalous. Jesus is saying that those who know *Him* know Yahweh. He claims He knows God the Father. That is not a passing comment or a statement listeners could be on the fence about. They had to decide either, *This is true, and now I have to live my life like it's true.* Or, *This guy is dangerous and out of His mind, and we have to get rid of Him.*

That choice to reject or accept the truth of God runs from cover to cover in Scripture. In His teaching in Matthew, Jesus alludes to Jeremiah 6. In that passage, the prophet Jeremiah warned Jerusalem of disaster to come. The people rejected God and turned to their own ways—and there were consequences. Then the Lord said in Jeremiah 6:16:

> "Stand by the roads, and look,
>> and ask for the ancient paths,
> where the good way is; and walk in it,
>> and *find rest for your souls.'*
> But they said, 'We will not walk in it.'"

The people in Jeremiah's day rejected God and chose to walk a different way. And Jesus reminds His hearers in no uncertain terms that many of them are doing the exact same thing. They could have had rest for their souls. But they said no.

Are we doing the same?

Finally, Jesus gives His invitation, the words many of us know and love—but words I often struggle to believe: "'Come to me, all who labor and are heavy laden, and I will give you rest. Take my yoke upon you, and learn from me, for I am gentle and lowly in heart, and you will find rest for your souls. For my yoke is easy, and my burden is light'" (Matt. 11:28–30).

> The yoke of Jesus comes not from an attempt at performance or perfectionism. It comes from mercy and love.

Usually, animals carried yokes, a beam attaching two animals pulling a cart or a plow. Sometimes, if a person was poor, they would carry that yoke on their own shoulders.[4] In Jesus' day, the Jews often spoke of carrying "the yoke of God's law and the yoke of his kingdom, which one accepted by acknowledging that God was one and by keeping His commandments."[5] Being a good Jew required you to carry this burden and subject yourself to the detailed restrictions laid out in the law.

While using similar language, Jesus offers a different way. He rejected the legalism and pride evident in many of the Jewish leaders. In Matthew 23:4, He even calls out the scribes and Pharisees when He says, "They tie up heavy burdens, hard to bear, and lay them on people's shoulders." But the yoke of Jesus does not do this. The yoke of Jesus comes not from an attempt at performance or perfectionism. It comes from mercy and love. Jesus calls His listeners to give up the burdens they're carrying, to stop hitching themselves to exhausting and impossible standards of the law and of the culture. Instead, He's saying,

Here, I have something better. Hitch yourself to Me, and when you take up My yoke, when you go My way, you'll find what you need.

For those who want to listen, for those who want to understand, Jesus doesn't pronounce "woes" on them. It's as though He turns to this group, to the people so often overlooked, to the weary and humble and dependent, and He urges *them* to come. He invites them to receive all they need from the source itself—from Him.

Like the Lord said through Jeremiah, Jesus says here, *There's another way! You don't have to be so broken down in spirit, so soul-weary. Look where the good way is, and walk those paths. And there you'll find rest for your souls.*

LAY ASIDE EVERY WEIGHT

In the darkest days of battling depression, every day felt like it weighed a thousand pounds. I couldn't believe life with Christ meant carrying a burden that was easy and light. But through the help of counseling, medication, encouragement from friends, being reminded of truth by my husband, crying out to God, and digging into His Word, I started to release the burdens that weighed me down. I started to let them go little by little, and even when outside circumstances did not change, God lightened the load pressing against my soul.

This shift didn't happen overnight, and it wasn't easy. It was a battle—and often still is. For me, fighting that battle included getting help from a doctor and counselor. If you are struggling with depression, anxiety, or other mental health issues, *please get professional help.* This book addresses many of the spiritual burdens that weigh us down, but I am acutely aware that our mental health and physical health play a huge role. It's all related, and I had to seek help to get my mind and emotions to a place where I could fight the spiritual battles I talk about in this book.

We have a God who doesn't leave us to our own devices, and He promises to provide what we need. Sometimes that means He gives us the help of skilled professionals, and we have the freedom to wisely and thoughtfully use those resources (more on this in chapter 5).

Looking back, I remember thinking those dark days felt as though Satan had thrown me to the ground and was pressing his foot into my back, shoving me into the earth. I faced a battle between truth and lies, a battle to fend Satan off from standing haughtily over me as though he had some kind of victory over my life, a battle to stop carrying burdens far too heavy for me.

The truth is that there is no lighter burden than what Christ gives us. Even so, we heap weight after weight upon our backs—burdens we were never meant to carry. *And we're exhausted because of it.*

It's time to take those off. Our souls are weary from carrying worry, carrying self-condemnation, carrying perfectionism. What would it look like if we threw off all those weights? What would it look like to live life *knowing*—beyond the shadow of a doubt—who God is and trusting what He says is true?

I think we'd experience a lot more joy, even in heartache. We'd experience a lot more freedom, even when we have work to do. We'd experience a lot more contentment, even in times of need.

Letting go of our burdens doesn't mean we will never have suffering and sorrow. We will mourn and lament. We will grow tired in this life because we are finite people living in a fallen world. But this is what Paul was getting at when he wrote from prison, "I know how to be brought low, and I know how to abound. In any and every circumstance, I have learned the secret of facing plenty and hunger, abundance and need. I can do all things through him who strengthens me" (Phil. 4:12–13).

There is no easier burden, no lighter yoke, than to be able to walk through life fully assured of the truth of who God is, what He says about you, and what He has called you to do.

NO LIGHTER BURDEN

A few years ago, my dad wrote an update for family and friends about my mom, Charlotte. It was right before Christmas, and at the time, she was dying of cancer. He wrote this:

> Charlotte is sleeping quietly now as I try to keep occupied with the day in and day out routine of being a caregiver. . . . I must admit I'm struggling. Winning and losing on the athletic field in high school and college, USMC boot camp, one year in the middle of an ugly war, raising six kids, trying to calm hurting fellow believers at church, ten years of business financial struggles—nothing hurts as much as watching the love of your life slowly deteriorate.
>
> I don't know how else to express it. Each day Charlotte needs a little more help with some of the very basics. One day she gave me a quote from C. S. Lewis, "We are not necessarily doubting that God will do the best for us; we are wondering how painful the best will turn out to be."[6] I wonder what He is doing, but I know He has the best in store for us. There is the greatest comfort of all. . . .
>
> How painful will the best turn out to be? I don't know, but I'm so glad that both Charlotte and I have that assurance that He knows, He cares, and He loves us with an infinite love.[7]

That is what letting go of our unnecessary burdens looks like. It looks like letting go of fear and worry and clinging desperately—even through tears—to the assurance that God knows, He cares, and He loves us with an infinite love. It looks like supernatural peace and abiding trust in our Father. It's believing, as Charles Spurgeon said, "We have all things and abound; not because I have a good store of money in the bank, not because I have skill and wit with which to win my bread, but because the Lord is my shepherd."[8]

Jesus invites us—the weary, the tired, the discouraged, the broken down—to come to Him and place our burdens at His feet. In the following chapters, we'll look at how we can do this. How can we begin to let go of what's weighing us down? Then in the final chapter, we'll see that when we rid ourselves of those unnecessary burdens, we can fully—and even joyfully—bear what we *are* meant to carry. When we let go of what's tangling us up, we can run with endurance, carrying our cross and carrying each other's burdens as we are called to do.

As Jeremiah wrote, *that* is the good way. That is the path we can walk, the way we find rest for our souls.

REFLECT

1. What's wearing you down right now? What burdens weigh heavy on your soul? Family struggles? Insecurity? Health problems? Injustice? Fear for a loved one? Your own failure? Bring those things before God. If you need help putting your cries into words, read and pray through passages such as Psalms 27, 55, or 130.

2. Consider your answer to question one. Envision being able to throw off those burdens, not in careless apathy, but in a way that entrusts them to God. Do you think anything would change in your day-to-day life? Would you be able to sleep better? Feel less stressed? Start taking care of yourself? Begin asking for help?

The point is not that we can guarantee outcomes or dream our wishes into reality. But we can often get so wrapped up in the burdens we're carrying now that we lose sight of the available peace, joy, rest, and strength we could be experiencing.

Chapter 2

WORTHLESSNESS

Created by a
God Who Loves You

*I praise you, for I am fearfully and wonderfully made. Wonderful
are your works; my soul knows it very well.*

* PSALM 139:14

Like you, I was made carefully, by a God who loved what He saw.

* DANIEL NAYERI

ONE CHILD SCREAMED WHILE the other two fought. Or maybe two
screamed while one complained. I can't recall all the details. I just remember telling my husband, Colson, I needed a break. I couldn't handle
the noise and chaos, so I held back tears, muttered a few words to him,
and walked out the door.¹

I wasn't leaving in any real sense, just searching for a few moments
of peace. I sat in the only place I knew would be quiet—in my car, in the
garage. With a few walls between my children and me, I could finally
hear myself think. I could finally try to still my soul.

But sometimes outer quietness reveals the inner storms.

I kept the car turned off and the garage door closed. I could still hear the muffled noises of my family inside, but I escaped the responsibility of listening to their cries and answering each sound. I thought I'd find calm in the dark, quiet garage, but my heart raged inside me. Sure, I could hear myself think—but I didn't like what I heard.

Lies about my parenting, my worth, my abilities, and my failures swirled in my head. I ruminated on how I'd yelled at my kids just ten minutes earlier, punishing myself with an inner monologue of how I was incompetent as a mom, a disappointment to my husband, my kids, and even to God. I was sure any love they had for me was mingled with a bitter taste of resentment.

I had failed so often, and while any one of those failures might not have looked like much to the outside eye, I knew the sum of them. I knew how much I yelled, how much I ignored my family, how I failed to live up to my expectations. I saw how my struggle with depression spilled over onto my kids. My heart broke every time they asked, "Why is Mommy crying again?" and I couldn't shake the guilt I felt when I'd excuse myself from the dinner table, leaving my husband to clean up the emotional mess I left.

I sat in the darkness of my garage, piling on the rebuke, the lies, the criticism. The weight of it all nearly flattened me.

And I wondered if I should just go ahead and turn the car on.

The idea stayed with me longer than I care to admit. I had everything I could ever ask for. The chaos in my home was chaos I'd dreamed of for years—the pitter-patter of tiny feet, family eating around the table, kids who make me laugh. But there I sat, weeping and wishing I could disappear altogether. I mulled over my options, and death had almost seemed like a good one. At that moment, I didn't act on my morbid fantasy, thanks to a healthy fear of dying and a support system I knew would be waiting for me on the other side of the garage walls. Still, I felt shaken, like someone was shaking me awake. Like there was a burning fire I'd long denied just outside my door. I'd smelled the smoke before, but I never thought I was in any real trouble. Until now.

I no longer thought, "I'd never do that. I'd never take my life or leave my family." Instead, I shook my head and quietly confessed to myself and to God, "I get why people do that." I understood why people, even those whose lives seem wonderful and perfect and #blessed, would throw it all away. My mind entertained thoughts I never imagined I'd have. *If I stay in this place for too long, will the next time end differently?*

My forehead rested on the steering wheel, my shoulders shaking from crying. I felt so distant from the God I'd walked with almost my whole life, so joyless and trapped. I felt worthless. And I believed the lie echoing in my mind: *They'd be better off without me.*

Hunched over, I wept until the tears dried up. Then I lifted my head, opened the car door, and stepped back into the safety of my house, to the sounds of my kids running and laughing like every other day.

That day, I didn't have a light bulb moment or a spiritual vision. I didn't suddenly feel close to God. But a glimmer of hope flickered in my soul, a remnant of truth reminding me escape was not the answer. Giving up didn't have to be the best option. Help was available,* and this feeling of worthlessness was a burden I did not have to carry.

OUR FICKLE SENSE OF WORTH

As I've wrestled with understanding my own worth, I've heard a lot of self-positivity messages reminding me no matter my body type, job, parenting style, or social status, I'm valuable and "worth it." In many ways, it's refreshing. We see posts on social media or even in advertisements

---

* *If you are struggling with depression, anxiety, or other mental health issues, please contact a licensed therapist or medical professional. If you are experiencing suicidal thoughts or are in emotional distress, please dial 1-800-273-8255 or 988 to be connected to the suicide prevention lifeline.* God in His grace has given people the ability to create resources like medication and counseling to help us, and I strongly believe we have the freedom to use those resources when needed.

saying we're valued just as we are—and that's true. But what our culture doesn't answer—at least sufficiently—is *why*.

Why are we valuable? Because unless we understand the why, those messages eventually ring hollow. Maybe Instagram tells us we're valuable, yet that same app is a catalyst for so many of us feeling like we never measure up. A motivational speech is great at first, but like a sugar-high, it wears off. We can repeat mantras all we want, but unless those mantras are built on a strong foundation of truth, they'll eventually fail us.

A surface-level pep talk isn't enough to save you when you're contemplating turning your car on while sitting in a closed garage. We need lasting truth to sustain us and remind us we have inherent worth and value not just because we say so—but because *God* says so.

Still, for so many of us, our sense of worth is as fickle as a toddler's eating habits. One minute, we're confident and hopeful, the next we're insecure and despairing. We might not care about having the most money or the most power or the most perfect life. But we at least want to be on par with everyone else. We at least want to feel competent.

Our worth is measured by the God who created us, the one who formed us in His image.

Even shooting for a standard of competence leaves us feeling "less than." We're frazzled and fatigued with our two kids, but when we look at the mom who seems to effortlessly raise six, we pile on the self-criticism. When a friend reaches another career milestone and we're still plugging away at our dead-end job, we let our apparent lack of accomplishment get to us. When we can't check off those boxes on our to-do list because depression presses us once again into our bed, we sink further into self-loathing. When we watch people get the marriage, the family, the job, the life we've longed for, our resentment grows.

But what if we believed our worth cannot change, no matter what happens or even what we do?

Our worth is not measured by our output. It's not measured by how much we accomplish or the job we have or how many kids we raise or how mentally or physically capable we are.

Our worth is measured by the God who created us, the one who formed us in His image, who loves us with an unconditional, never-ending love, and who invites us to be His children.

CREATED IN HIS IMAGE

In their creation stories, many ancient Near East cultures depicted gods who created solely for themselves; humans served as slave labor for the gods. One commentator wrote, "In the Babylonian tradition man is created to alleviate the manual burden of the gods and provide food for their sustenance; men and women are mere slaves who survive at the whim of the deities."[2]

But that's not who our God is! That's not what He did at creation. Genesis 1:27 tells us, "So God created man in his own image, in the image of God he created him; male and female he created them." Genesis 1 goes on to say that God blessed them and told them to be fruitful and multiply, and He provided food to sustain them and for them to enjoy (Gen. 1:29). And then He calls His creation of humans not just *good*, but *very good* (Gen. 1:31).

This truth is mind-blowing, especially when compared to other creation stories. God provided for His people, not the other way around. He gave them abundantly more than they needed for survival. He *blessed* them (Gen. 1:28). The true Creator God created for His glory and for the enjoyment of humans who were formed in His image. Old Testament scholar John H. Walton wrote, "In the Bible the cosmos was created and organized to function on behalf of the people that God planned as the centerpiece of his creation."[3]

Adam and Eve were not an afterthought when God spoke the universe into being. They weren't a utilitarian necessity like other ancient stories depicted. Humans were—and are—creation's *centerpiece*, the finishing touch, the crowning glory, the very image of God Himself.[4]

In the same way, you are not an afterthought. You are not an accident or a mistake. You are not forgotten by God or left by Him on the bottom shelf of His creation. You do not need to prove your worth by your looks or your accomplishments or your performance or even your impeccable theology. You're already His image bearer, intricately formed by the powerful and loving hands of a God who sees and knows every part of you.

We are fearfully and wonderfully made through this intimate act of creation that calls us to praise:

> Wonderful are your works;
>   my soul knows it very well.
> My frame was not hidden from you,
> When I was being made in secret,
>   intricately woven in the depths of the earth.
> Your eyes saw my unformed substance;
> in your book were written, every one of them,
>   the days that were formed for me,
>   when as yet there was none of them. (Ps. 139:14–16)

You, too, are a centerpiece of creation, one who has incalculable value because you were molded with intention, love, and care by the Creator of the universe.

HE LOVES US UNCONDITIONALLY

Luke wrote a story of a group of Pharisees and religious leaders at a dinner party. They're reclining around the table, discussing the minutiae of the law in between bites of bread and sips of wine. Simon, the host, sees a woman from the corner of his eye. His jaw tenses. *What is she doing here?* The conversation stops as the rest of the group looks in the direction Simon has been glaring. *That woman showed up?! She needs to go, now!*

She's the one with the reputation, the one known around town for living a sinful life. Others are gathered outside the house listening to the intellectual conversations taking place among the Pharisees in attendance. Somehow, she managed to make her way through the crowd and toward the party.

But because of her sin, this woman is unclean. Her poor reputation precedes her, and she, of all people, should not be there.[5]

Then she walks up to Jesus, Simon's guest. She stands behind Him as He reclines at the table. And she weeps. She bends toward Him, letting the tears fall on His feet. Then she takes her hair and wipes the tears away.[6] Everyone there cringes and gasps—everyone except Jesus. Any respectable woman would not ever think of letting her hair down or touching a man like that in public.[7] But then again, she is not a respectable woman.

She keeps crying. Maybe she's embarrassed at this point— embarrassed by her reputation, embarrassed she cried in front of Jesus, embarrassed she acted on this crazy impulse to approach the Teacher. But she can't help herself. She takes the ointment she has and anoints Jesus' feet.

People stare, their jaws nearly touching the floor. Maybe they're thinking, *Why is He letting her do this? She's unclean, and she can make those around her unclean.*

Simon says to himself, "If this man were a prophet, he would have known who and what sort of woman this is who is touching him, for she is a sinner" (Luke 7:39). Jesus should know, but apparently, He doesn't. To Simon's mind, Jesus must not be a prophet.

Simon doesn't see. He doesn't recognize Jesus' power when it looks like humility or His compassion that appears shameful. Jesus tells a story and puts Simon in his place. *Simon, you gave me no water for my feet, no kiss, no oil for my head. But look at what this woman has done!* "Therefore I tell you, her sins, which are many, are forgiven—for she loved much" (Luke 7:47).

Jesus turns to the woman. I imagine His eyes are filled with compassion, His mouth curves into a smile. There's no hint of insincerity in His voice, no disclaimers attached to what He tells her next: "Your sins are forgiven. . . . Your faith has saved you; go in peace" (Luke 7:48–50).

Who is this man who thinks He can forgive sins? they murmur. This work of Jesus is scandalous, even blasphemous to them.

He is God Incarnate, the Messiah, the Servant about whom the prophets spoke. Yet Simon and the Pharisees can't see grace through the scandal. They can't see the image of God through the woman's sordid reputation. They can't see that her worth isn't bound up in her ceremonial cleanliness or understand how God's love doesn't depend on her ability to keep the law.

Her worth was decided by her Creator, and God's love for her depended on who *He* is, not who she was.

This sinful woman poured her burden of worthlessness out at the feet of Jesus. Unlike Simon, Jesus is too good, too kind, too loving to heap it back on her. Instead, He welcomes her. He forgives her. He commends her for her faith. And He sends her home in peace.

While I haven't carried the reputation she did, I have wept before Jesus. He has never rejected me. Sometimes, He seems silent.

Sometimes, I resist coming to Him. Sometimes, I still fear a look of disappointment in His eyes.

But when I read of how He treated sinners, outcasts, and children, as well as all those who are beaten down and on the fringes, I'm struck by His responses. He called people to repent of their sin, and He rebuked the arrogant and self-righteous. But His words and actions reflect the love of the Father. He's not a compassionless taskmaster. He cares deeply for us. He wants us to come to Him with our burdens so we can walk home at peace.

> **If we know and believe God's love for us, we cannot at the same time believe we are worthless.**

As with the sinful woman in Luke, Jesus doesn't shame us. He doesn't throw up His hands in disappointment or roll His eyes when we cry at His feet. He doesn't call us worthless or a lost cause or beyond redemption.

Instead, Jesus demonstrates in His life and ministry the character of Yahweh. He is love in human form, demonstrating to us the truth told to the Israelites in Exodus 34:6: "The LORD, the LORD, a God merciful and gracious, slow to anger, and abounding in steadfast love and faithfulness."

We cannot exhaust the love of God. He is *abounding* in it, overflowing because it is His very essence—and what we do cannot change that. Yahweh tells His people of that love in Exodus and throughout the Old Testament, despite their waywardness and disobedience. Jesus showed that love to the sinful woman, even though she had quite a past. And God demonstrates that love to us "in that while we were still sinners, Christ died for us" (Rom. 5:8).

Do we believe that? Do we trust God when He continually reminds us of His love for us?

If we know and believe God's love for us, we cannot at the same time believe we are worthless. The apostle Paul wrote, "For I am sure that neither death nor life, nor angels no rulers, nor things present nor things to come, nor powers, nor height nor depth, nor anything else in all creation, will be able to separate us from the love of God in Christ Jesus our Lord" (Rom. 8:38–39).

Even in the depths of our sin, our failure, our inability, our weaknesses, our exhaustion, God still loves us with an unconditional, never-ending love.

HE INVITES US TO BE HIS CHILDREN

I used to have this recurring daydream that played in my mind especially on dark, discouraging days. I pictured walking toward Jesus, seeing Him from a distance, and nervously—but excitedly—moving toward Him. I wanted to crawl in His lap, to soak up His love and grace, His mercy and compassion. But as soon as I got close to Him, my countenance changed as I looked at His face. I stopped—puzzled and saddened—a few feet short of where He sat. I didn't crawl into His lap. Instead, I awkwardly shifted my weight and hung my head lower and lower with every passing second. He looked straight at me, then looked at the ground, shook His head, and walked away.

This image felt so real, so indicative of how I viewed myself and Jesus. I longed for Him to say, "Well done," but I believed instead I'd be a disappointment, not even worthy of an explanation. He'd only shake His head and turn back, throwing up His hands that this worthless woman would dare to approach Him.

But that is not who Jesus is. Unlike the distant deities in ancient Near East culture, the one true God actually cares for the people He created—to the point where He sent His Son to die for us and invites us to be His children.

When my own kids come to me for help or simply to be near me, I too often can get annoyed at the interruption. I don't want to have to repeatedly answer the same questions about having a snack or how to spell "animal" or why they need to share. I can easily dismiss their needs and fail to welcome them because it's inconvenient and I am selfish.

But we are not interrupting God's work when we come to Him. He's not annoyed when we pray or ask for the same thing over and over. He doesn't resent our tears, and He's not threatened by our questions.

Oftentimes, I believe I must have used up His patience, wearing Him out with my pettiness and disobedience. But God's love never runs dry, and He never tires of us coming to Him.

John 1:12 says, "But to all who did receive him, who believed in his name, he gave the right to become children of God." When we confess our failures and our waywardness and believe that our healing comes only through the life, death, and resurrection of Jesus, we are saved—and not just saved from peril, thrown on a lifeboat, and then forgotten. We're *children of God*, saved and called to live as citizens of His kingdom. While we'll share in suffering in this life, we also get to enjoy all the rights, privileges, and even the inheritance that comes with being His child.

Paul says it this way in Romans 8:14–17:

> For all who are led by the Spirit of God are sons of God. For you did not receive the spirit of slavery to fall back into fear, but you have received the Spirit of adoption as sons, by whom we cry, "Abba! Father!" The Spirit himself bears witness with our spirit that we are children of God, and if children, then heirs—heirs of God and fellow heirs with Christ, provided we suffer with him in order that we may also be glorified with him.

We can approach God as a loving, gracious, generous, forgiving Father. We can cry out to Him, and He won't dismiss us as if we're a kid annoying a parent. And one day we will fully reap the benefits of being an heir in the kingdom of God—a kingdom that will never be shaken (Heb. 12:28).

HE DECIDES OUR WORTH

When I sat in my car that evening years ago, lies rang loud and clear in my ears. *I'm not good enough for my family. Look how much I've messed everything up. No one wants to be around me.* The evil one would love us to fall for his deception. He wants nothing more than to leave us wallowing in our misery, paralyzed by this burden of worthlessness.

As soon as we become Christians, we "become the special objects of the attention of the devil," wrote Martyn Lloyd-Jones, a twentieth-century Welsh preacher, minister, and medical doctor. "It is because we belong to Him that the devil will do his utmost to disturb and upset us. He cannot rob us of our salvation, thank God, but while he cannot rob us of our salvation he can make us miserable."[8]

The clichés of our culture will never be strong enough to battle an enemy intent on breaking us. But the devil cannot sway us when we're firmly rooted in the truth. When we know we bear God's image, when we're fully assured of His love for us, when we stake our lives on the reality of being His child, and when we trust Him as a perfect Father, we can find rest. We can find the strength to take another step, even when life becomes impossibly hard. We can know the "peace of God, which surpasses all understanding," and see how that peace truly does guard our hearts and our minds (Phil. 4:7).

Our culture, our family, our friends do not decide our worth. Even we do not decide our worth. As the one who formed every bone in our body and every hair on our head, God gets to decide.

And He has declared you His image bearer, a person deeply loved by Him, and through Christ, He has even declared you His child.

REFLECT

1. Do you ever struggle with feeling worthless? Do you ever feel like you're a disappointment to God or to others in your life? When have you felt like that and what was it that stirred up those feelings?

2. Imagine yourself humbly approaching Jesus the way the sinful woman did in Luke 7. Do you believe, deep in your soul, that He'd respond to you the way He responded to her? Or do you tend to think He'd reject you, shame you, or ignore you?

3. Which truth do you struggle to believe the most—that you are created in the image of God, loved by God, or are invited to be a child of God? Why?

4. Today, what would it look like for you to take a first step to lay aside the burden of worthlessness?

   If you need a place to start, consider reading through Psalm 139, the story of the sinful woman in Luke 7:36–50, or Romans 8.

Chapter 3

CONDEMNATION

The Accuser Will Not Win

Who shall bring any charge against God's elect? It is God who justifies. Who is to condemn? Christ Jesus is the one who died—more than that, who was raised—who is at the right hand of God, who indeed is interceding for us.

> • ROMANS 8:33–34

If you are in Christ—and only a soul in Christ would be troubled at offending him—your waywardness does not threaten your place in the love of God any more than history itself can be undone.

> • DANE ORTLUND

AFTER LUNCH, I SET my twins up in the basement to watch a movie, so I could give my two-year-old a bath.[1] He seemed to wear summer all over his body. As I wiped off the jelly, dirt, and sweat from my little boy, I heard a knock at the front door. I didn't answer, figuring it was Amazon or maybe a door-to-door salesperson.

Another knock.

I stood up from where I knelt beside the tub and glanced out the window. The woman who had knocked was heading back to her car. *I guess it wasn't anything important*, I thought—until I watched her turn and walk back toward my house.

I wrapped my son up in a towel and carried him downstairs so I could answer the door.

"Hello?" I called as she returned to my front steps. "Can I help you?"

"I just had to grab my ID badge."

Huh? I scrolled through my memories trying to place this woman. *Did I know her? Was I supposed to know what she was there for? Did I have an appointment I forgot?*

I held the door open for her, my face blank. With her badge in hand, she walked right into my house, as if she had a right to be there.

"DCFS," she said.

Department of Children and Family Services. I don't even remember what she said next. "Umm, he just finished taking a bath," I said, wrapping the towel more tightly around my son. "Can you give me a minute?"

But before I could step away to get him dressed, she explained she was there to see what happened yesterday and to check on my son—and photograph his injuries.

The day before, that same towel-covered two-year-old had fallen from his second-story bedroom window—and I was still reeling from it. The hospital told us even though he wasn't seriously injured, it was protocol to report the incident to DCFS. I knew we'd be contacted by them. I didn't realize, however, that the procedure required an unannounced home visit within twenty-four hours.

The woman was cordial enough as she lifted up the towel he still wore and took pictures of his scrapes and bruises. Miraculously, those were the extent of his injuries. I walked her through the house, stepping over the embarrassing mess of toys and dirty laundry strewn across the floor. I tried (unsuccessfully) to keep from crying while she took pictures of the window he managed to unlock, and I wondered if she believed that yes, indeed, my two-year-old really did open the window on his own.

Soon after, she walked down the steps to the basement where the twins were nestled on the couch. I paused their movie, and she asked me to leave the room so she could talk to them without any risk of me monitoring their answers. Later, she questioned me, asking if I had mental health issues and the dosage of the medication I took. Admitting depression is one thing. Being humiliated by it is another.

"What are you going to do to make sure this doesn't happen again?"

I had already ordered child safety locks for the windows, frantically googling the best and safest ones with the highest reviews. I tried to think of anything I could say in this moment to show I was an okay parent: *I've set up a follow-up appointment at the pediatrician's office. I'm adding another childproof lock to the front door to be extra cautious. I have additional personal references I can send if needed.* I don't even know if what I said made sense. I felt dizzy, my mind spinning with memories of picking my son off the dirt below his bedroom window, just a few inches from a piece of concrete. More tears fell as I tried to present myself to be as capable a mom as possible.

She talked me through what would happen next, the personal references I needed to submit, the rights I had as a parent. Then she handed over a few papers. The title of the first one seared into my brain: "Notification of Suspected Child Abuse and/or Neglect Document."

She asked a few more questions and left me with pamphlets about the investigation process. My hands clenched those papers as I repeated *Don't cry, don't cry, don't cry* in my head. I reminded myself to breathe and walked her out the door. She took a few final pictures of the mangled shrub that broke my son's fall. The concrete right next to it still haunts me.

When she finally climbed into her car, I closed the front door and ran to find my phone. I called my husband sobbing. My words were a jumbled mess. I collapsed on the couch with my head in my hands, wiping tears off my phone with the hem of my shirt. Despite knowing this visit was protocol and knowing my son was safe, the intensity of the scrutiny undid me. While my son walked away from that fall with a clear CT scan and only a couple of scrapes and bruises, I walked away shattered.

I wasn't entirely surprised we ended up in the emergency room with my third kid. He is the most adventurous one, the curious one, the mischievous one, the one who can figure out how to open or press or unlock almost anything. But I always thought an ER visit would come after a fall at the playground or something more "normal." I did not think he'd find his way out of a locked, second-story window. And while I am far from a perfect parent, I did not, in a million years, think I'd be investigated for abuse or neglect.

Later that night, I couldn't sleep. I replayed the accident over and over in my mind, scrutinizing the answers I gave to the social worker's questions. I wondered what my twins told her (they later told me they talked about their birthday party). I stared at the ceiling trying to keep the sounds of my sobs down, but the image of finding my son on his back in the mulch and the images of what could have happened were burned into my brain. After a couple hours, I got out of bed, walked into the spare bedroom across the hall, and wept.

At four in the morning, Colson came in—I hadn't hid my crying so well. He sat across from me while I buried my face in my hands and, for the hundredth time, grieved how our son could have died. I should have kept a closer eye on him. I should have put childproof locks on his windows. I should have known better. I should have done better. I should have just *been* better.

We lucked out, I told myself. But I failed. *Who lets their son fall out a two-story window?* I was a failure. A terrible mom. And now a stranger documented my nightmare on a stack of forms, my performance as a mother placed in a folder to be analyzed.

Colson listened while I released my thoughts and fears like a dam breaking. My body shook and the tears would not stop as my mind envisioned what could have happened. And based on what could have happened, I deserved, well . . . my thoughts spiraled down into darkness.

"They'd be better off without me," I mumbled. The phrase I'd spent months wrestling through in counseling, months working to counter with truth now rang too loudly to ignore. *This incident happened under my watch. I blew it as a mom. My kids are worse for it. They're worse off because of me.*

"You're believing lies. But what's actually true?" Colson asked.

I couldn't answer.

I sat in the dark, only a sliver of light from the hallway peeking through the door, while my husband helped me dismantle falsehoods and fight against the lies clawing at my heart. I cried while he spoke truth over me, truths I kept trying to refute, because the lies were so deeply etched in my mind.

Yes, it could have been worse, he told me. *But you are not a failure as a mom. God is still in control. We cannot protect our children from every single thing. God is still good. You're not guilty of the allegations being investigated. God has been and always will be faithful, even if we can't always understand His ways.*

Eventually my breathing calmed and my tears slowed. Truth started to hush the lies, at least enough where I could crawl back into bed for a few hours of sleep. Colson would have to keep reminding me of those truths over the following weeks as I mentally relived my son's fall and dealt with the follow-up DCFS visit and phone calls. But God pulled me, little by little, out of my own darkness. He took off the weight of condemnation that was crushing me.

SORTING OUT TRUTH FROM LIES

Whether it's parenting challenges, failures in my work, marriage, or other relationships, the devil has found a way to whisper—and sometimes shout—accusations in my ear. Maybe you've heard them too. We can all too easily believe phrases like *I'm a failure, I'm not good enough, people will resent me, my kids are better off without me, I'm a terrible friend, I can't believe I messed up like that again,* or *why do I even bother trying.* And when we believe those lies, we're unable to rest in the grace and forgiveness of God.

It gets especially complicated, though, because sometimes there are pieces of truth mixed in with the lies. We have messed up. We have failed. Maybe some people do resent us. We're not always a good friend. Sin comes all too easily to us, and often we do need to confess. If we're honest, we know we've fallen short and missed the mark. How do we sort out the lies when the accusations seem to be true?

Eugene Peterson wrote in *A Long Obedience in the Same Direction,* "The lies are impeccably factual. They contain no errors. There are no distortions or falsified data. But they are lies all the same, because they claim to tell us who we are and omit everything about our origin in God and our destiny in God."[2] There may be truth in Satan's accusations. But he conveniently leaves out the reality of our redemption.

Other times, we listen to the condemning words of others, our culture, our own expectations, and we let those words take root in our souls even though they're not even remotely true. Maybe we don't do what someone else wants, and we blame ourselves for their response. Or an unavoidable accident happens, and the consequences eat away at us. Or maybe hard circumstances leave us in an endless cycle of "I should haves." *I should have said something differently. I should have prepared better. I should have seen that coming.*

The devil has a thousand tricks up his sleeve, ways he reminds us that we deserve darkness instead of light, death instead of life—and he's right in some ways, isn't he? He can name real sins and shortcomings and point out how we are undeserving of the life God offers. So, lies and the truth get muddled together, twisted and warped, and we struggle to keep it all straight. We might know "for all have sinned" (Rom. 3:23) and "the wages of sin is death" (Rom. 6:23), but some of us get stuck there. We forget what comes next in those verses. We see only our faults, and so we repeat words of condemnation and phrases of judgment like a broken record, wincing as the scratches rhythmically remind us of our own brokenness.

We end up being so sure of our failures, yet so unsure God's grace is enough to cover them.

CLOTHED IN HIS RIGHTEOUSNESS

The condemning accusations of Satan are nothing new. He's been whispering deceit since he spoke to Eve in the garden, and he's been accusing the people of God for thousands of years.[3] In the book of Zechariah, the prophet gives us a picture of what Satan seeks to do—and what God has done instead.

Zechariah's prophetic ministry took place in the postexilic period, the time following the Jewish people's return to their land after having been exiled in Babylon for decades.[4] In chapter 3, he records a vision that happens in a heavenly courtroom. The angel of the Lord stands in front, in the place of judgment. Joshua (not the one from the book of Joshua), the high priest of the day who represented all of Israel before God, faces him. At Joshua's right hand, in the typical place of accusation under the law,[5] stands Satan.

Satan hurls accusations at Joshua, naming all the things he's done wrong—and everything Israel has done wrong. As the one standing before God on behalf of the people, Joshua's status of guilt isn't just about him. If he is found guilty in this heavenly courtroom, that means all of Israel would be found guilty. Satan knows this. He knows how much the people have messed up. They've just returned from exile, a period in their history serving as divine punishment—and look at Joshua! He is representing Israel? He's covered in filth (Zech. 3:3). He showed up before God literally in excrement-covered clothes.[6] *The priest of God is covered in sewage.* He's obviously "unclean," impure according to the law and therefore unable to be in the presence of a holy God. Satan is not about to let this slide.

But the Lord steps in. He rebukes Satan, shutting him up from speaking accusations that, by the looks of it, are all too true.

> And the angel said to those who were standing before him, "Remove the filthy garments from him." And to him he said, "Behold, I have taken your iniquity away from you, and I will clothe you with pure vestments." And I said, "Let them put a clean turban on his head." So they put a clean turban on his head and clothed him with garments. And the angel of the LORD was standing by. (Zech. 3:4–5)

There is nothing you or I could do to undo the work of our Savior.

Satan is right when he points out the filth that covers Joshua. He's right when he accuses Israel of her sin. But that does not stop the Lord from being merciful and gracious and kind and forgiving. God does for Joshua and the people what they could never have done for themselves, transforming him and Israel from shame to glory, from unclean sinners to those clothed in the righteousness of God. Satan's accusations are meaningless and powerless before a gracious and all-powerful God.

That same God who cleansed Joshua cleanses us. On our own, we stand before God filthy, covered in a mess of our own making, and He has every right to turn His face from us, every right to condemn us right then and there. Instead, He takes off our filthy rags and clothes us in righteousness, a righteousness we could never muster on our own but comes only from God Himself (see Phil. 3:8–11).

Zechariah's vision points us to the cross. The priest, Joshua, had the promise of the coming Messiah, he had the assurance that God would one day bring His servant, "the Branch," to wipe away the iniquity of the community *in a single day* (Zech. 3:8–9). God's people before Christ longed for this day and held on to the promise God made. We get to look back at the fulfillment of it, the moment when Jesus cried, "It is finished."[7] On that day, Christ didn't dismiss the accusations as baseless but took all that condemnation upon Himself. No matter our past, no matter our faults, no matter our mistakes, He took all of them to the cross. *It really is finished!* And there is nothing you or I could do to undo the work of our Savior.

THE PARDON OF OUR PRINCE

In his allegorical book *The Pilgrim's Progress*, John Bunyan wrote the story of Christian, a man who journeys from the City of Destruction to the Celestial City. Along the way, Christian comes to the cross where the heavy burden (representing sin) he has carried falls off. The journey is still hard and dangerous, but because of Christ's death on the cross, Christian is able to continue without the weight of that sin.

Shortly after, Christian meets a character named Apollyon who claims to rule over the City of Destruction. Apollyon threatens Christian for leaving his kingdom then tries to lure him back to Destruction. But Christian professes loyalty to a new king who promises deliverance and eventual glory. Apollyon scoffs, accuses Christian of his faithlessness, and recounts his every misdeed along the journey: He fell asleep when he should have kept watch. He didn't always trust God. He tried to rid himself of his burden through means other than the cross and nearly gave up when he saw lions along the way. He proved himself faithless and unworthy to receive whatever this ruler of the new kingdom had to offer. There's no way, Apollyon reminds him, that Christian belongs in the Celestial City. He belongs with other sinners, with those who live in the City of Destruction.

But Christian responds, "All this is true, and much more which thou has left out; but the Prince, whom I serve and honor, is merciful, and ready to forgive; but, besides, these infirmities possessed me in thy country, for there I sucked them in; and I have groaned under them, been sorry for them, and have obtained the pardon of my Prince."[8]

When I read that story, I laid the book down on my lap and sighed an "Amen" with tear-filled relief. I've been in the church all my life, but something about the way Christian fought back against the evil one with the truth of his redemption hit me in a new way. We are faithless and fallen. We are easily distracted and too often doubting. Sometimes, false accusations are thrown at us, and we must battle against them and wrestle with what it means for God to be just. Other times, we're accurately accused of very real failures. But no matter his tactic, the devil, when he reminds us of the lies, leaves out the part about being pardoned. Christian knew so many of Apollyon's accusations were true—but he also knew a greater truth: *he had already obtained the pardon of his Prince.*

First John 1:9 says, "If we confess our sins, he is faithful and just to forgive us our sins and to cleanse us from all unrighteousness." We, too, can receive the pardon of our Prince. We can carry the yoke of grace instead of condemnation, life instead of death, glory instead of shame.

When we do that, we're free to grieve our sin without fear, and we can have holy sorrow for our failures. We know the grace of God. We don't abuse that grace by continuing to live in sin. That would be like wearing an outfit covered in sewage when God has given us new clothes or submitting "to a yoke of slavery" after we've already been set free (Gal. 5:1). But when we're free from the burden of condemnation, we're also free to parent, to love, to work, to live God's way with joy, knowing the accusations of the evil one hold no power over us. Like Joshua the high priest, we get to give up our filthy rags and "put on the Lord Jesus Christ" (Rom. 13:13–14).

Paul says in Colossians 2 that we were dead in our trespasses, but God made us alive "by canceling the record of debt that stood against us with its legal demands. This he set aside, nailing it to the cross. He disarmed the rulers and authorities and put them to open shame, by triumphing over them in him" (Col. 2:14–15). We do not bear the shame of our sin anymore. It's been nailed to the cross, and Satan himself has been defeated.

I don't know what words of condemnation nag at you. I don't know your story of failure, if there's a moment when you let someone down, a day when you felt like the worst parent on the planet, a constant feeling of guilt you carry. But I do know this: we can be free from the burden of condemnation because no failure is too much for the grace of God.

THE ACCUSER WILL NOT WIN

I could sit and analyze over and over again that day my son fell—and I have. I tend to overanalyze nearly all my failures and beat myself up for them long afterward. But God has been reminding me of the truth of His grace, and I can tell you there is nothing more freeing, more joy-inducing, more soul-filling than being able to say with assurance, "There is therefore now no condemnation for those who are in Christ Jesus" (Rom. 8:1). *None.* None! Can you believe it?

There's a scene in the book of Revelation that may help put the final nail in the coffin of our condemnation. The apostle John sees a vision of the angel, Michael, fighting against a great dragon (Satan). Revelation 12:9–11 says:

And the great dragon was thrown down, that ancient serpent, who is called the devil and Satan, the deceiver of the whole world—he was thrown down to the earth, and his angels were thrown down with him. And I heard a loud voice in heaven, saying, "Now the salvation and the power and the kingdom of our God and the authority of his Christ have come, for the accuser of our brothers has been thrown down, who accuses them day and night before our God. And they have conquered him by the blood of the Lamb and by the word of their testimony, for they loved not their lives even unto death."

As much as we battle with the evil one this side of eternity, in the end, *the accuser will not win.* In fact, because of the resurrection, he's already lost—and he knows his time is running out. In the meantime, he will do everything he can to destroy the people of God. Yet the blood of the Lamb leaves Satan with no basis for his accusations.[9]

Athanasius, a theologian and church father from the fourth century, when talking about the death of Christ, encouraged his readers by saying, "Have no fears then. Now that the common Savior of all has died on our behalf, we who believe in Christ no longer die, as men died aforetime, in fulfillment of the threat of the law. That condemnation has come to an end."[10]

> Whatever you've done, whatever accusations you hear or condemnation you carry, they are no match for the reality of the cross and the empty tomb.

On our own, we will never be able to answer Satan's accusations with a sufficient defense. But the death and resurrection of Jesus answers for us. Because of our Savior, *our condemnation has come to an end.* Death itself, Athanasius went on to point out, "has become like a tyrant who has been completely conquered by the legitimate monarch . . . conquered and branded for what it is by the Savior on the cross."[11] If death itself has no hold on us, what power do the allegations of the evil one still have?

Even the apostle Paul, the Pharisee who, as Luke put it, "ravaged the church," dragged followers of Jesus from their homes, threw men and women in prison, and approved of the brutal execution of a man named Stephen,[12] asked rhetorically in Romans 8, "Who is to condemn?" Friend, like Paul, I pray all of us can shout with holy confidence, "No one!" Because Christ Jesus died, was buried, rose from the dead, sits at the right hand of God, and intercedes for us (Rom. 8:34).

Whatever you've done, whatever accusations you hear or condemnation you carry, they are no match for the reality of the cross and the empty tomb. They are no match for the blood of the Lamb and the power of a gracious Savior who now sits on the throne. Christ has won. That is the truth we can cling to until the end, the testimony we have, the easy yoke we get to carry.

REFLECT

1. When have you heard words of condemnation? What lies even if there's a grain of truth in them—have you wrestled with?

2. What does resting in the grace and forgiveness of God look like? Is it taking a step of faith to accept the grace God offers through the life, death, resurrection, and exaltation of Christ? Pray through the words of 1 John 1:9, confessing your sins and trusting that God is faithful and just to forgive you. He wants to take your filthy garments, like those of Joshua, and give you new, clean robes—new life.

Maybe you need to wrestle with failures in your past and speak truth over them. Maybe you need someone else to speak truth over you, like my husband did for me, because condemnation rings so loudly in your own ears. Confess what needs to be confessed. Reach out to a trusted friend or a counselor to speak truth over your life.

Remember, the accuser will not win. New Testament scholar G. K. Beale wrote that despite our ongoing earthly battle, "we now have all the resources of heaven open to us, the same resources that hurled the enemy down to earth in the first place."[13]

Satan's lies hold no power over us when we trust the God who has already triumphed over him.

Chapter 4

WORRY

Not Afraid of Bad News

"Therefore I tell you, do not be anxious about your life, what you will eat or what you will drink, nor about your body, what you will put on. Is not life more than food, and the body more than clothing? Look at the birds of the air: they neither sow nor reap nor gather into barns, and yet your heavenly Father feeds them. Are you not of more value than they?"

* MATTHEW 6:25–26

Underneath human anxiety is the reversal of identity in which the finite attempts to be infinite. With our finite knowledge, we want to know everything so as not to be caught off guard by anything. With our finite abilities, we want to try to control everything so we're not controlled by anything. We fail to do both because it's impossible to be like God in this way, making the peace of God elusive for those who need it most. But behold Jesus. He is forever settled, unshaken and unbothered to the point that He can sleep like a baby while a storm rages war on his resting place.

* JACKIE HILL PERRY

WE PULLED SEVERAL FAKE leather chairs into a circle in the corner of the hospital lobby. A Christmas tree glimmered in the center of the room and carols playing over the speakers. My dad, a few of my siblings, and our spouses recalled the events of the last couple days—the sudden yellowing of my mom's skin, the Christmas celebration we moved two days early before she was admitted to the hospital, the Buddhist doctor willing to perform surgery on December 25. Extended family and friends trickled in over the course of the morning, providing everything from sandwiches to prayers.

After several hours, the surgeon walked through the double doors to our left and made his way toward us. We stood up, both eager for an update and entirely unprepared for his words. "We got everything we saw," he said, his voice calm and matter of fact. He paused, giving us a moment to savor the comfort of his last sentence before delivering the next one. "But it looks like it's pancreatic." *Pancreatic cancer . . .* a diagnosis often requiring some mix of invasive surgery, chemotherapy, radiation. And still, there's a low survival rate.

I don't remember much about the rest of that day. At some point, my siblings and I went back to our parents' house and microwaved chili from the freezer, set the dining room table, and ate a very different Christmas dinner than we expected. Later that night, I lay in a guest bed next to my husband and sobbed. My mind reeled with the news, still processing what had happened and now picturing her stitched up and recovering in a sterile room under fluorescent lights. *Would the cancer come back? What would chemo do to her? Would she recover from surgery? How am I going to go back to work after this? What's Dad going to do?*

Grief entered our home that week like an unwanted guest we couldn't evict. But worry snuck in the door too. The fear of what *could* happen, sorrow over a *potential* future scared me almost more than the heartache of the present. Grief felt heavy on its own, but worry felt like a boa constrictor, tightening around my mind and heart until I could barely breathe. Any semblance of joy and peace I once had became suffocated in its grip.

But how do you just *stop* worrying? How do you sit in a hospital waiting room without worry pulling up a chair next to you? How do you live in a season filled with unanswered questions and waiting and uncertainty? How do you walk through a pregnancy after multiple miscarriages or look at your shrinking bank account compared to your growing bills and *not* worry? Or watch a loved one make poor choice after poor choice, read the day's headlines, or drop your kid off at college—without worry coming along for the ride?

TURNING OUR GAZE TO GOD

I'm a worst-case scenario thinker, prone to worry about any number of issues, such as the outcome of major surgery or meeting deadlines or my kids falling off their bikes. Worries often plague my soul, and I struggle to escape them. In the Sermon on the Mount, Jesus told His listeners, "So do not worry about tomorrow, for tomorrow will bring worries of its own. Today's trouble is enough for today" (Matt. 6:34 NRSV). *Do not worry*. It sounds so simple, doesn't it?

The worry we're talking about isn't the same as thoughtful concern, care, or caution. The term, like Jesus used in Matthew 6, means "to have an anxious concern, based on apprehension about possible danger or misfortune."[1] The idea can even be expressed in some languages by phrases like "'to be killed by one's mind' or 'to be pained by thinking.'"[2] We play out all that could possibly go wrong and feel the pain of outcomes yet to happen. *Worry hurts.*

Yet flippantly telling yourself (or someone else), "Don't worry about it," doesn't often work. We can't *will* ourselves to not worry.[3] Believe me, I've tried. When Jesus told His listeners not to worry, He didn't offer that statement as a shallow sentiment. He told them not to worry—but He also reminded them right then *why* that's possible. There's no need to worry because of *who* God is: *He's the one who feeds the birds of the air. He makes the lilies grow. He even clothes the grass.*[4] He helped turn their gaze from their problems to their God.

When we're worried, we can all too easily lose sight of who God is. Maybe deep down we believe the problems we face are bigger than He is. Or we believe He's so busy dealing with the cosmic battle of good versus evil or the "big" issues in the world that He doesn't have time for the minutiae of our lives. Or maybe we know God is powerful and in control—but *He's* the one we're scared of. We worry about what *He* will do or allow. And so, we distance ourselves from our Maker, avoiding Him either consciously or subconsciously because we don't believe He's powerful, caring, or trustworthy.

But as I've wrestled with my own worries over the years, I've come back to the truth that there is no lasting peace, no freedom from worry, that comes apart from God.

NO PROBLEM BIGGER THAN GOD

The Israelites in the Old Testament often worried. When I think about the dangers and hardships they faced, I can't blame them. God miraculously delivered them from the hand of the slave-driving Pharaoh; but as they fled, they found themselves trapped between the Red Sea and Pharaoh's quickly approaching army. They panicked and cried out to Moses:

> "Is it because there are no graves in Egypt that you have taken
> us away to die in the wilderness? What have you done to us
> in bringing us out of Egypt? Is not this what we said to you in
> Egypt: 'Leave us alone that we may serve the Egyptians? For it
> would have been better for us to serve the Egyptians than to die
> in the wilderness.'" (Ex. 14:11–12)

Despite the miraculous works they had witnessed—like the Nile River turning to blood and God leading them as a pillar of cloud and a pillar of fire—the people could not fathom how to escape what they now faced. Behind them, an angry and humiliated Pharaoh chased them with a vast army of chariots and military officers, and in front stood an impassable body of water.

Moses responded, "Fear not, stand firm, and see the salvation of the LORD, which he will work for you today" (Ex. 14:13). *Don't worry! Not because the dangers we're stuck between aren't real—but because the Lord can and will save.*

Moses stretched out his hand over the sea, and the waters parted in two. The people walked through on dry ground, a wall of water on their left and one on their right. When they were all safely on the other side, the Egyptians still in hot pursuit, Moses stretched out his hand again and those walls of water came crashing down. The Israelites watched in awe as God saved them from their enemies.

Can you imagine seeing this? Can you imagine your reaction when Moses first says, "Fear not!" I'd shake my head and roll my eyes and yell, "Yeah right, Moses! Are you in denial about what's happening?" Of course Moses wasn't in denial. No one could ignore how big their problems were—but God was bigger.

Our worries can seem vast when they're all we see. But when we take those worries and compare them to our God? No contest. After the parting of the Red Sea, Moses and the people burst out in song, "I will sing to the LORD, for he has triumphed gloriously; the horse and his rider he has thrown into the sea.... Who is like you, O LORD, among the gods? Who is like you, majestic in holiness, awesome in glorious deeds, doing wonders?" (Ex. 15:1, 11). *No one.* There is no one like our God, no problem beyond what He can handle.

After being rescued from Egypt, you'd think the Israelites would have learned their lesson. Yet not long after, while journeying through the wilderness, they grumbled because they lacked drinkable water.

They worried about dying from thirst, and yet again, God saved them, miraculously making the bitter water sweet (Ex. 15:22–25). They panicked when their stomachs growled in hunger, telling Moses and Aaron they would have preferred God to kill them in Egypt (Ex. 16:2–3). Then God provided manna from heaven. And then *again* when they were thirsty, they complained. But still, God gave them what they needed (Ex. 17:1–7). He continually made good on His promise to Israel, leading them into the land flowing with milk and honey.

Time and again, the Israelites fixed their eyes on their worries instead of their God. They were distraught and scared, unable to imagine how God could possibly solve all their very real and very hard problems.

We do the same, don't we? Sometimes we get so focused on what we can see that we lose sight of the hope we have in what is unseen. We forget we serve the same God who parted the Red Sea and provided manna from heaven. He's our Creator and Sustainer, the one who calmed storms and raised the dead. If He has that kind of power, then "is anything too hard for the LORD?" (Gen. 18:14).

Our need to feel safe is real and good and valid, and our fears and worries alert us that something's off. But instead of being consumed by our worries and fears, those things can nudge us to find safety in our God.

TAKING OFF OUR EVERYDAY WORRIES

For many of us, being stuck between a threatening army and a huge body of water isn't a typical worry. Most days, we're knee-deep in diapers or bills or an out-of-control email inbox we can't seem to tame. We come to God with our big worries—the diagnoses, the heartbreaks, the major decisions. We believe the stories of Scripture, and when we're truly desperate and out of options, we'll get on our knees before the all-powerful God. But our everyday stresses? Our very "normal" fears? We can (and are supposed to) handle those on our own . . . right?

Eugene Peterson wrote:

We know that God created the universe and has accomplished our eternal salvation. But we can't believe that he condescends to watch the soap opera of our daily trials and tribulations; so we purchase our own remedies for that. To ask him to deal with what troubles us each day is like asking a famous surgeon to put iodine on a scratch.[5]

Many of us carry around a thousand small worries, fears we hold inside our hearts and our bodies that, maybe on their own, don't seem like a big deal. Until eventually, our knees begin to buckle under their weight. We've walked with those stresses on our backs for so long, adding another to the pile each day and believing God is just a little too big to intervene in our ordinary lives.

But Jesus says we get to take the weight of those worries off too.

If you were to write down every single thing you worry about, what would be on that list? Maybe your paper would be filled with to-dos you fear you won't have time to finish or how you'll meet that deadline when your childcare falls through. Some of us worry what others think of us and fear making a bad impression. We're plagued with the fear of being a disappointment, and so we strive endlessly to please, wearing ourselves ragged in the process.

We worry about what our kids are being exposed to at school, how we'll come up with money for an unexpected car repair, or if a friend misinterpreted our text. We worry about how we'll be able to resolve the fight we had last night with our spouse or why a family member isn't returning our call (and if you're like me and automatically assume the worst, you start to believe "tragic car accident" must be the answer to that last one).

For me, one nagging worry I've carried over the past decade has been our paycheck. Since before we were married, my husband's job has been 100 percent commission based. Each paycheck can fluctuate dramatically from month to month. Through circumstances beyond our control, there were even several months in 2012 when that paycheck went to zero (literally) overnight. God must have known I needed to work on trusting Him with this area of my life, because while there are no guarantees in any job, my personality would much prefer our family to live with a regular nine-to-five position with a steady paycheck.

In some ways, we've gotten used to the ups and downs of work. And when I put this all in perspective, we have it easy. We have financial safety nets in our family and community. We have a roof over our heads and more than enough food on our table. I'm not exactly an Israelite wandering in the desert, grumbling from near starvation.

Yet, I still worry.

Part of the issue with these everyday worries is that sometimes, we don't realize we're worried at all. Recently, my husband and I had to make decisions about our health insurance, and I had no idea how stressed I felt until I broke into tears mid-conversation. The worries we hold on to will come out eventually, a geyser erupting through means like sleeplessness, bursts of anger, health issues, or unexpected crying. If we want to find rest for our souls, if we want to have freedom from fear, we have to first *name* our worries. We have to stop what we're doing long enough to consider, "What's weighing on me? What am I *actually* worried about here?" Otherwise, those worries sit in our minds like a dying rodent in our attic—unnoticeable for a while and seemingly small. But unless that animal is found and removed, the stench will worsen, affecting us and anyone around us.

Too many of us ignore these small worries instead of bringing them before the only One who can bring true peace. God is working in grand and miraculous ways throughout the world, but even the Great Physician wants to tend to our every scratch.

First Peter 5:7 tells us that we can cast all our anxieties on God, "because he cares for you." "Casting" in that verse means to throw something on someone else. In the Greek, it's an idiom communicating the idea that what you're casting is someone else's problem now. You're giving up responsibility and putting it on them.[6] *All* our worries, *all* our anxieties and ordinary stresses, we get to take these off our shoulders and throw them on God. Unlike us, He can bear the weight. Our worries won't give Him stress headaches or cause Him to lose His temper. The sovereign God can carry it all—and He is *willing* to carry it all. Why? Because He cares.

When warning them about inevitable persecution, Jesus told His disciples, "Are not two sparrows sold for a penny? And not one of them will fall to the ground apart from your Father. But even the hairs of your head are all numbered. Fear not, therefore; you are of more value than many sparrows" (Matt. 10:29–31). Most of us will not face the level of violence and persecution the disciples faced, but the truth about who God is remains the same. The God who numbered the hairs on your head also cares about your paycheck, your back pain, your fear of flying. He cares how your kids are doing in school and how you struggle with people-pleasing. He wants you to lay those things down before Him, to heap them on *His* back because He loves you. And everything that weighs on your soul matters to Him.

WHEN WE'RE AFRAID OF WHAT GOD MIGHT DO

Six months after my mom was diagnosed with cancer, I pulled my phone out of my pocket as it buzzed. My shoulders slumped as I saw my parents' number. By that point, I dreaded when they called. It often seemed to be bad news, and even if it wasn't, talking to them reminded me how hard things were at that point for my mom. This time, though, it wasn't about her.[7]

My dad's recent blood work looked concerning to his doctor. I remember walking from a coffee shop to my office at the time, and after

I hung up the phone, I threw up my hands and yelled, "Here we go again."

Doctors soon diagnosed my dad with cancer—multiple myeloma, a relatively treatable kind, they assured. Despite a decent prognosis for him, both my parents spent the following months undergoing varying levels of treatment. My siblings and I swapped off helping out, and I flew from Chicago to New Jersey as often as I could to do my part. I sat with my mom during chemo and "worked from home" in my dad's hospital room. I occasionally went to an oncology appointment with them—a joint appointment, because when you both have cancer, why not schedule your doctors' visits together?

God appeared to answer my cries about my mom with more grief. I asked Him to heal, and it felt like He heaped on more sickness instead. *What's the point of coming to God if He's not going to do anything—and especially if He's going to allow the situation to get worse?*

Sometimes, we're scared of what God will do if we hand over our fears. We'd rather hold on to our worries than cast them on a God who can, at least to us, seem unpredictable at times. We're terrified He'll answer in ways we don't want. Dallas Willard wrote, "I believe that one of the reasons we resist fully surrendering our lives to God is the fear that he might allow desolation in our lives."[8] We're afraid of God. We're afraid His yoke won't actually be easy, His burden won't actually be light. *If I totally surrender my life and my plans to Him, what will He do?* We're nervous to pray, "Your will be done,"[9] because Jesus prayed that prayer, and it led to His gruesome death. And so, as author Paul Miller put it, "We prefer the safety of isolation to engaging the living God."[10]

Many of us are afraid to approach God with our worries, because, deep down, we don't completely trust Him.

When my parents were both sick, I wrestled with whether I could trust God. I questioned His ways and lamented like the psalmist, "Why, O LORD, do you stand far away? Why do you hide yourself in times of trouble?" (Ps. 10:1). God sometimes seems silent. We're on our knees begging Him to work, and it doesn't seem like He even cares enough to show up. Or maybe it feels like our lives are too mundane and insignificant for our proverbial paper cuts to matter when He's busy restitching the world.

When Jesus' mother and disciples watched Him die a criminal's death, it seemed like God didn't make good on His promise to redeem and deliver His people. He failed. He was silent. This man who was supposed to be an answer to Israel's bondage, to all the prophecies of the Old Testament, hung on a Roman torture device. Then the supposed Messiah lay in a tomb while His disciples hid in fear. The people had cried to the Lord for generations, and apparently, He didn't answer. Where was God?

The burden of worry doesn't need to have a hold on us because not even the grave had a hold on Him.

He was about to raise the dead.

Author Tish Harrison Warren wrote that we can wait on God, keeping watch even in the darkness "because the things I long for are not rooted in wishful thinking or religious ritual but are as solid as a stone rolled away."[11]

The burden of worry doesn't need to have a hold on us because not even the grave had a hold on Him. That reality is the linchpin of our faith, the truth we have to decide whether we believe. If the resurrection is true, then God can be trusted—even when we sit in the darkness and the unknowns, even when His solution to our brokenness is the broken body of His only Son. As Paul said, "He who did not spare his own Son but gave him up for us all, how will he not also with him graciously give us all things?" (Rom. 8:32)

FIGHTING WORRY THROUGH PRAYER

My dad has often told the story of how my grandmother used to pray while he was deployed to Vietnam as a helicopter pilot. Time and time again, she'd fall on her knees in her room, her hands outstretched and her head bowed low before God. Her worries were legitimate; my dad's return in a flag-adorned casket was a very real possibility. I can only imagine how all-consuming her worry would have felt. But my grandmother also knew prayer was the only antidote to her worry. She had no control, no way to ensure my dad's safety, no minute-by-minute updates on whether he was still alive. The only thing she could do was cry out to God.

We cannot live a life without worry unless we're living a life of prayer. Prayer is *how* we cast our cares on God, and sometimes doing so involves serious lament and wrestling with Him. It's not a light switch we turn on and suddenly we're worry-free. But through prayer, we can find the safety and comfort we need in the presence of our good and loving God. We can come to Him daily, regularly, and even flat on our faces. In moments of desperation or when we have no other words, we can pray simple sentences like: "Spirit, give me wisdom." Or "Lord, have mercy." Or "God, help my unbelief."

God doesn't guarantee the answers we want. But through prayer, He reminds us who He is. He reminds us of His power and His care. He reshapes our own hearts and convicts us through the Spirit when our worries are a result of our own self-imposed stress or entitled attitude. He gives us space to lament, to approach Him with our questions— even with our anger.

Paul wrote in Philippians:

> The Lord is at hand; do not be anxious about anything, but in everything by prayer and supplication with thanksgiving let your requests be made known to God. And the peace of God, which

surpasses all understanding, will guard your hearts and your minds in Christ Jesus. (Phil. 4:5b–7)

God is near, the time when Christ returns is coming—and He will make all things new. In the meantime, we don't have to be stuck in the mire of worry and fear. Instead, our anxieties can prompt us to go to God and seek the peace He offers.

Psalm 112:7 says, "He is not afraid of bad news; his heart is firm, trusting in the LORD." I want to live like that, don't you? When we gaze at our God instead of our problems, when we unclench our fists and heave our worries on God, when we stop pulling on our bootstraps and instead fall into the arms of our Savior, we can find rest. It's not because we've finally gotten all our ducks in a row, or our plans A through Z written down, typed up, and laminated. We do not have to fear bad news because of *who* God is—a powerful God who cares deeply for us and is perfectly and always trustworthy.

REFLECT

1. What are you currently worried about? Name all of it, writing down every fear or worry that comes to mind.

2. What holds you back from being free from worry? Do you struggle to believe God is all-powerful? Do you feel like your worries are too small for God to care about? Do you have a hard time trusting Him with your fears because you're scared of what He'll do?

   We can find rest from fear and worry when we see God for who He truly is. He is holy, good, and loving. He is gracious and powerful, sufficient, compassionate, and perfectly loving. As the apostle John wrote, "There is no fear in love, but perfect love casts out fear" (1 John 4:18).

3. The writer of Hebrews said, "For we do not have a high priest who is unable to sympathize with our weaknesses, but one who in every respect has been tempted as we are, yet without sin. Let us then with confidence draw near to the throne of grace, that we may receive mercy and find grace to help in time of need" (Heb. 4:15–16).

Spend time in prayer, bringing your list of fears and worries before the throne of grace.

Chapter 5

SELF-SUFFICIENCY

You Were Made to Be Dependent

I lift up my eyes to the hills. From where does my help come? My help comes from the LORD, who made heaven and earth.

* PSALM 121:1–2

Autonomy and self-sufficiency are finally postures of hopelessness in which free gifts are excluded and one is left to one's own resources.

* WALTER BRUEGGEMANN

I SAT PERCHED ON THE STAIRS with my ten-month-old squirming in my arms, one toddler on the toilet upstairs, and one on the toilet below on the main level. From this spot, I could keep my twins in view, and they could hear me call out, "You can do it!" or "Just try for one more minute!"

I put off potty-training my twins for months after they'd shown signs of being ready, trying to avoid the inevitable messes and hassle.

Eventually, the cost and exhaustion of three kids in diapers provided enough motivation for me to start. I knew it'd be hard, but hey, my mom did this with six kids. *It can't be that bad.*

During the week, I read a book on potty training. On Thursday morning, I put away all the extra diapers in the house that weren't for my youngest. By Monday, I resolved, my twins would be diaper-free. (You can see where this is going, right?)

At the end of day one, I called my sister, Jenn, in tears. "I need help!" I told her. I'd been on my hands and knees wiping up pee every few minutes, the baby kept wanting to play in the toilet, and I barely had a moment to scarf down leftover chicken nuggets for lunch. I was desperate and depleted.

The next morning, she pulled into my driveway. *Help is here!* I gave her the quick rundown of our progress (or lack thereof), and we got to work. She kept an eye on the baby, put dirty dishes in the dishwasher, and made peanut butter and jelly sandwiches for lunch. I returned to my seat on the stairs—now able to give my attention to my two half-naked toddlers.

Even though my twins had all of me, there were still *two* of them. So, while I helped wipe and care for my daughter on the main level, my son was on his own upstairs. Which was fine, until, "MOOOOMMY!"

I sprinted up the stairs to find him in tears, yelling, "My loveyyy!" As soon as I came into view of the bathroom, my eyes bugged out of my head. Water cascaded out of the toilet like a fountain, soaking the bathmat and spreading onto the rest of floor. And it would not stop. His little stuffed puppy he'd snuggled since infancy lay on the floor, in danger of drowning according to the imagination of my son. But the much bigger problem was the reality that water would soon leak through the floor, then through the ceiling below—right onto our kitchen table.

"Jenn! Get towels!" I screamed while I ran to grab the plunger. (Thankfully, the overflow was mostly due to too much toilet paper.) I got the toilet to stop overflowing. Jenn ran up the stairs with a fresh batch of dry towels. And I tried to console my son, "It's okay, Bud. We'll just wash him. Puppy Lovey will be fine."

As my sister kept mopping up water, I carried a load of sopping towels downstairs to the laundry room—and saw that the overflow had leaked to the ceiling below and now needed to be dried out, patched up, and repainted. All I could think was, *I didn't sign up for this.*

When we finally got the kids settled, the water cleaned up, laundry going, and leaked-on furniture sanitized, my sister and I looked at each other—and started laughing hysterically. We tried to compose ourselves, but every time we talked, we couldn't stop chuckling. My house was still a mess, my ceiling would need repair, and my toddlers remained half-clothed.

That moment, standing in my kitchen cracking up at the chaos, felt a whole lot different than the day before when I sat alone, unable to stop crying because of how overwhelmed I felt by this very normal parenting task.

ADMITTING OUR NEED

I'd like to think of myself as a relatively competent person. I'm not the best or the worst. When I played soccer in college, I made the team— but then sat on the bench. I can read music and carry a tune, but no one should ever hire me to perform. I can cook, but I certainly won't be receiving a Michelin star anytime soon. I resonate with that saying, "Jack-of-all-trades, master of none." For the most part, that's good enough for me. I can read, research, or try hard enough, and eventually I'll be able to figure things out by myself . . . or so I used to believe.

But nothing has stripped me of my sense of competence more than motherhood. Whether it's potty training or talking to my kids about a difficult topic or remaining patient when everyone is driving me bonkers, parenting has made me realize I'm not nearly as competent as I once thought. Just a couple days ago, when working through a challenge with one of my kids, I blinked back tears and whispered to the other grown-up in the room, "I have no idea what else to do."

Most, if not all, of us have experienced some situation in our lives where we can't manage everything on our own. Our struggle may not be with parenting but with a job we don't feel qualified for or a relationship issue we can't solve. No plan or list or talent we possess seems to help, and eventually, we have to admit we're out of ideas, energy, brainpower, and skill. On our own, we're stuck. But that's a good thing.

When we let go of trying to be sufficient in and of ourselves, we're free to receive help from God, ask for help from others, and utilize the resources God has enabled people to create.

TURNING TO THE ALL-SUFFICIENT GOD

There's a story in the book of Isaiah about Hezekiah, king of Judah, coming to the end of his rope. Sennacherib, king of Assyria, was invading Judah. An Assyrian high official came to Jerusalem, Judah's capital city, to taunt the people and convince Hezekiah to surrender. The official said to the people, "Do not listen to Hezekiah. For thus says the king of Assyria: Make your peace with me and come out to me. . . . Beware lest Hezekiah mislead you by saying, 'The LORD will deliver us.' Has any of the gods of the nations delivered his land out of the hand of the king of Assyria?" (Isa. 36:16, 18). The Assyrians were strong, and they knew it. They had already taken over other cities in Judah. Hezekiah had even tried to strike a deal with Sennacherib, paying him silver and gold (including silver and gold from the temple) to get them to withdraw (see 2 Kings 18). But still, Assyria determined to take hold of Jerusalem and defeat Judah.

When Hezekiah heard about the threats from the Assyrian official, "He tore his clothes and covered himself with sackcloth and went into the house of the LORD" (Isa. 37:1). Tearing clothes and putting on sackcloth demonstrated distress, repentance, and humility. One commentator remarked, "At last Hezekiah realized that the Lord was his only resource and at once turned to him."[1] Despite being the king of Judah, all Hezekiah could do was fall to his knees in desperation, pleading with God to intervene. No amount of wealth, no strength of his army, no strategy worked in the face of a vicious enemy. Only God could deliver them—and He did. Because of Hezekiah's desperate prayer about Sennacherib, God defended the city of Jerusalem and sent an angel to save Judah by miraculously striking down 185,000 Assyrian soldiers (Isa. 37:21–38).

All Hezekiah had—power, an army, the resources of a kingdom—was insufficient. Only by turning to the all-sufficient God could he find what he needed.

We so often pat ourselves on the back for being self-sufficient, for being able to figure out solutions or meet needs on our own. It's good and right to have a sense of responsibility and ownership over the choices we make and the ways we solve problems. Yet too often, we rely on our own abilities *instead* of on God. We want to try our solutions first, without His help—and only when we're truly desperate, we'll come to Him. Thankfully, like with Hezekiah, He's gracious and compassionate, and He helps us in our time of need.

> **What if we sought God *first*, before we drained ourselves and our resources?**

But what if we did things the other way around? What if we sought God *first*, before we drained ourselves and our resources? What if we asked for His help on a regular, daily basis, seeking wisdom from the Holy Spirit and provision from our generous Father?

Our problems wouldn't necessarily disappear; God never promised they would. But how different it would be to walk through hard situations *with* our God instead of digging in our heels and declaring like a toddler, "I do it myself!" God is ready and willing to generously pour out wisdom on us, to lead us in "paths of righteousness" as David wrote in Psalm 23. He desires that we come to Him because He is our help, the all-sufficient God who created us to depend on *His sufficiency*—not our own.

My dad ran track and played football in college, served as a Marine Corps helicopter pilot in Vietnam, earned his MBA, ran a business, raised six kids, eventually retired to be a full-time pastor, and was married to my mom for nearly forty-seven years until she passed away. Long story short—my dad is a good, competent man.

As a kid, I'd walk into my dad's study to ask a question or tell him my latest news. Especially if it was first thing in the morning or late at night, I'd often find him on his knees, arms propped up on the seat of the armchair, and head bowed. The minute I noticed his posture, my body would freeze, and I'd tiptoe back out of the room. Walking over the threshold of his door felt like stepping onto holy ground. Even as a little girl, I knew he was talking to God. I wasn't about to interrupt the conversation.

There is nothing like watching a good, competent man on his knees in prayer, aware of his need and imperfection. Even if I couldn't articulate it at the time, I knew the source of his wisdom and integrity. My dad exemplified a lot of admirable traits when I was growing up— and he still does. But there has been nothing more formative to me than seeing him exemplify a need for Jesus.

Our needs will always outweigh our competence and self-sufficiency. Like Hezekiah, when we finally recognize our need, we end up in the best place—on our knees before our God. And that's the posture we should have started with in the first place.

IT'S OKAY TO ASK FOR HELP

A few years ago, Colson took a day off work to help me at home.[2] I'd been struggling with anxiety and depression, and me calling him midday on the verge of tears wasn't uncommon. But usually, after I vented and he gave me a pep talk on the phone, I could find a way to power through with the kids until he returned in the evening. This particular morning began as normal, with diaper changes and sippy cups of milk. But by 8 a.m. it spiraled into kids crying and my taking a timeout behind my bedroom door. A pep talk wasn't enough. I needed help, space, an extra set of hands, and someone with the patience I lacked.

Not long after my desperate phone call, my whole body relaxed when I heard the garage door open. Colson had arrived back home to take over for me. For the rest of the day, I saw him take the kids to the park, make their lunch, and put our two-year-old down for a nap. I felt guilty that I didn't contribute and guilty that he carried the load of two parents. Rather than being grateful for my husband and his flexible job, I resented needing the help.

I'd tell anyone else it's good to ask for help. For me, it's even okay if I ask for help in the obvious "all hands on deck" situations—like having twins, a rough bout of the flu, or the death of a loved one. I'll happily meet you at the door to take a casserole off your hands or let you play with toddlers while I recover from a C-section. But on an average Tuesday when I just can't pull it together? That doesn't reach my standard of a "good reason" to call in reinforcements.

The day I called my husband for help, an internal war waged between what I knew in my head to be true and the lies hounding me every moment. *You're not a good mother. You're weak. Everyone else seems to be able to handle this—and more—on their own. What's wrong with you?*

I've resisted this lesson for years, but I'm slowly starting to grasp that asking for help doesn't mean I've failed—it means I'm human. We were not created to be self-sufficient; rather, God meant for us to depend on Him *and* other people. After He created Adam, God said, "It is not good that the man should be alone, I will make him a helper fit for him" (Gen. 2:18). Our need for others even predates sin entering the world. God designed humans to live in community. In other words, *we don't have to do life all on our own*. We were never meant to.

There are times when the amount of help we need may not be available, and we don't always have the luxury of calling for backup in the middle of the day. But more often than not, many of us don't even bother to ask, either because of pride or not wanting to inconvenience others or a failure to recognize our need. Yet no matter how competent we think we are, there will always be walls we can't break through. We can choose to keep hammering away by ourselves, growing more breathless with every swing. Or, we can look around at the people and resources in our lives, ask for what we need, and choose to be grateful when someone answers.

DEPENDING ON EACH OTHER WITHIN THE CHURCH

When our twins were about five months old, Colson flew to California to visit his brother. I promised him I could survive without his help for a couple of days. On Sunday morning, I ventured to church by myself— my motivation mostly being the fact that I could hand my infants off to the nursery workers for an hour and sit in the service without someone clinging to me. I unloaded my babies from the car and walked toward the church door practically doing bicep curls with a car seat in each arm. After about five steps, one of the men from our church saw me, sprinted out to the parking lot, asked if he could take the car seats, and carried them all the way to the nursery for me. It was a small gesture, one I didn't even ask for. I *could have* done it on my own. I was strong and healthy enough to carry my kids where they needed to go. But the relief I felt when he freed my aching arms was about far more than the physical weight being lifted.

I found a spot in the sanctuary, and as I sang along to the hymns, I realized, "If something happened to Colson, I would be okay." It's a grim thought, for sure, and the grief of losing him would be shattering. But in the long run, we'd make it. With my husband traveling and two little babies at home, I carried an underlying fear of what I'd do without him.

Yet, in that moment, God reminded me I *had* help. I looked around the church and saw people in my life who wouldn't just carry car seats— they'd carry me.

In John 13:35, Jesus said to His disciples, "By this all people will know that you are my disciples, if you have love for one another." He doesn't say the world will know we're His disciples by our perfect theology, our capabilities, our political affiliations, or the quotes we share on social media. The world will know that we follow Jesus *because we love one another.*

In Acts, Luke records how the early church put this into practice. They were not self-sufficient but depended on each other:

> Now the full number of those who believed were of one heart and soul, and no one said that any of the things that belonged to him was his own, but they had everything in common. And with great power the apostles were giving their testimony to the resurrection of the Lord Jesus, and great grace was upon them all. There was not a needy person among them, for as many as were owners of lands or houses sold them and brought the proceeds of what was sold and laid it at the apostles' feet, and it was distributed to each as any had need. (Acts 4:32–35)

The church is a community of broken people redeemed by Jesus and given the task of demonstrating the kingdom and character of God on earth as it is in heaven. But, unfortunately, many of us have experienced churches where we cannot be honest about our brokenness. We cannot ask for help without feeling shamed. We witness division, harsh rhetoric, finger-pointing, and defensiveness instead of self-giving love. The church can (and often has) too easily become a bunch of homogenous communities placing higher priority on preferences, programs, or even wielding power than exemplifying what God's kingdom is really like.

In Acts, the apostles gave "their testimony to the resurrection of the

Lord Jesus," and the truth of the resurrection led to a radically loving way of life within the community of believers. Love is how we live out our belief in Jesus' resurrection and our hope of the resurrection life to come. As N. T. Wright said, "Love is at the very heart of the surprise of hope: people who truly hope as the resurrection encourages us to hope will be people enabled to love in a new way."[3]

Our hope in the gospel and our worship of Jesus should propel us to love others in such a profound, undeniable way that people outside the church take notice—and maybe even *want* to be a part of it. Whatever our past church experiences, what would it look like for us to practice self-giving love from here on out? How can we, both individually and as local church communities, live out our resurrection hope in the way we love each other and our neighbors?

I read an article years ago about Francis Collins, world-renowned physician-geneticist and devout Christian, who debated and eventually befriended the late author Christopher Hitchens, a self-proclaimed "anti-theist." After Hitchens was diagnosed with esophageal cancer, Collins reached out to offer any support he could, including helping Hitchens wade through his medical options. When it came to their core worldview, these two men could not have been more different. But after witnessing the life and conduct of Francis Collins, Christopher Hitchens referred to him as "the best of the faithful." As one writer put it, "His affection for the man he once treated with disdain was undisguised."[4]

What if those who vehemently disagreed with us could not deny the faithfulness they saw in us? What if our love was so evident in our speech, actions, work, and daily lives that even the person most opposed to God couldn't help but lean in a little closer to witness what resurrection life looks like in action? What if Christians became known for the way they run to serve others, sprinting out to parking lots to carry babies, being the first to drop off a meal, speaking kind words even to someone who has hurt us, rallying around the sick, the hurting, and even those others think don't deserve our help?

The church should be the foremost place where we demonstrate we are not self-sufficient. The very gospel we proclaim says *we cannot save ourselves—and we don't have to.* Not only do we hold on to this belief individually by confessing our need for salvation and coming to Jesus daily, but we also live it out by loving one another as Christ has loved us.

USING THE RESOURCES GOD PROVIDES

We stood in the kitchen cleaning up after the kids were in bed. I leaned on the counter, and Colson and I returned to a conversation that had resurfaced a number of times over the prior months. Along with my counselor and my doctor, we'd been talking about whether I should start taking medication for depression, something I'd been trying to avoid and only entertained as a last resort.

"How do you feel about it?" he asked. I had a lot of thoughts, a lot of feelings, a lot of apprehension. My shoulders slumped, and I anxiously clutched the dish towel sitting next to me. I was scared it wouldn't work, that I'd be "unfixable," and I'd have to come to terms with the fact that the darkness I lived in was the new normal. I was nervous about side effects, the cost, the hassle of having to take a pill every day for who knows how long. But most of all, I felt like I'd failed.

I hated admitting I couldn't muster up the strength and energy to get over my depression. I hated that my efforts to exercise and eat right, while essential, weren't enough. I hated the fact that God didn't heal my mental struggles when I read and reread Scripture and cried out to Him. While I never would have faulted anyone else for taking medication, I hated confessing *I* needed it.

Sometimes, Christians (either consciously or subconsciously) believe that utilizing resources like counseling, medical care, support groups, or various kinds of therapy means we're not relying on God. We're not believing He's sufficient to heal or our faith is weak or there may even be unconfessed sin in our lives. Those things *can* be true, but

I've come to realize that it's the very grace of God that frees us to get all the help we need—from Him, from others, from the local church, even from the resources people in the world have created.

Most (if not all) of us are quick to get help for our physical bodies. We'd rush to the doctor to fix a broken leg, yet we can sometimes turn our nose up at the idea of getting help for less "acceptable" ailments like depression, anxiety, or addiction. We somehow believe we're calling God insufficient or we lack faith if we can't figure those things out on our own. But God's character is not tarnished because I take a pill every day to fight depression. Rather, His generosity and goodness can be seen in the help He provides through ordinary (and very smart) people. It's a lie that we're stronger people or stronger Christians if we forgo the tools at our disposal.

Psalm 121:1–2 says, "I lift up my eyes to the hills. From where does my help come? My help comes from the LORD, who made heaven and earth." Our help comes from God—and He's a God who cares enough to give us not only eternal salvation, but myriad resources to help us through our everyday struggles.

In February of 2020, I started taking medication for depression. The decision required discernment, prayer, and wisdom. That pill didn't solve all my problems or take away my need for Jesus and others. But it has been a gift from God. It has helped me think straight enough to do the work of counseling, read my Bible, and pray. I'm a better wife and mom. I'm able to parent and live and work in a way I couldn't when the cloud of depression loomed over me. I'm still alive because of it, and I thank God every day for His help in the form of a little green pill.

Self-sufficiency is a burden we don't need to carry. God is the only one who is fully sufficient, and He created us to live in community. He even enabled people in our world to create resources that help us mentally, spiritually, and physically. And we can take Him up on all those offers, because living out the gospel means we can admit our need, ask for help, and accept the generosity of God—in whatever form it comes.

REFLECT

1. Do you struggle with asking for help? What kind of help do you resist the most? Do you resist coming to God in prayer? Asking others for help? Taking a step to use other resources?

2. What does it look like for you this week to let go of the burden of self-sufficiency? Is it getting on your knees in prayer or seeking support from a friend? Maybe it's sending a message to the pastors of your local church to share your needs with them or finally making an appointment with a counselor.

   Getting help can be scary. We don't always know how others will respond. We don't know if a certain treatment will work. We can't predict what God will do. But trying to figure it all out on our own will only leave us isolated and burn us out. Asking for help is a risk worth taking—and we can trust that no matter what happens, the all-sufficient God will never leave us.

Chapter 6

INSECURITY

The Only Opinion
That Matters

*Those who look to him are radiant, and their faces shall never be
ashamed.*

* PSALM 34:5

*Through Jesus Christ, we are relieved of the burden of having to
prove our goodness, the weight of our rightness resting completely
on Him. . . . When we are no longer troubled with maintaining
our own goodness, we can partake of the goodness around us.*

* HANNAH ANDERSON

I WALKED OUT of the church building after a speaking event, and immediately, the knot in my stomach dissipated. As a novice speaker, I
could finally exhale knowing that while I had plenty of room for im-
provement, I hadn't made glaring errors or tripped while walking on
stage. There's nothing like the wave of relief that comes when you're
finally confident you didn't mess up *too* terribly.

I climbed into my car to head home. But before driving out of the parking lot, I looked up the livestream recording on my phone to text it to my husband. I fast-forwarded through the music until I came to the part where I stepped onstage. As soon as I heard myself talking, my heart sank. *No, no, no!* In the online version, the audio sounded like I'd been slurring my words. In the monitors on stage, everything had sounded fine—at least that's what I thought. But afterward in the recording, certain words sounded like my four-year-old was saying them. I was mortified. *Is this how I sounded to everyone watching online? This is so distracting! What will they think of me?* I desperately wanted to run back to the church and announce to everyone, "I don't actually sound like that!"

In reality, the audio issues that morning were nothing more than a minor hiccup, and I could have shrugged off the situation and learned from the experience for the next time around. But on my way home, I couldn't stop obsessing over what people thought, how they perceived me, and whether they would ever invite me back. It was as if someone had put a pin in the balloon of my already fragile self-esteem, and I became acutely insecure about my voice, my abilities, and my desire to teach the Bible.

In his book *Out of Solitude*, priest, theologian, and writer Henri Nouwen talked about how our culture can be so easily obsessed with superlatives. We want to be the best, the fastest, the brightest, he observed. But there's more beneath the surface of our striving. He wrote:

> But underneath all our emphasis on successful action, many of us suffer from deep-seated, low self-esteem and are walking around with the constant fear that someday someone will unmask the illusion and show that we are not as smart, as good, or as lovable as the world was made to believe.[1]

Isn't that the truth? Some of us (raising my hand right now) can be debilitatingly insecure. Any confidence we have in who we are depends largely on ever-changing opinions. As our feelings and others' views shift, so does our sense of security.

Have you ever left a friend's house and then immediately started to dissect every word you said? The wheels of overanalysis start spinning, and you berate yourself for being too loud, too shy, too quiet, too *whatever*. Your internal dialogue may have started with thoughtfully considering if you should have said or done something differently. But sometimes self-reflection runs wild, becoming an unhinged monster of self-critique we can't restrain.

Or maybe you want to do something God has called you to do, but then you get in your head about what others may think. Or you struggle to take compliments, shifting uncomfortably in your seat and trying to bat away kind words like a bug buzzing around your head. Some of us wear ourselves out with overwork or overcommitting, sacrificing sleep and sanity to an unhealthy degree, because what would people think if we said no to their requests? Other times, we struggle to admit our failures because maybe it would be better to sweep those under the rug if it'll help us avoid possible humiliation.

We can be trapped by the need to daily evaluate our performance, try to prove our worth (even to ourselves), or attempt to preserve our image. Like a tic we can't seem to control, we do things like refresh our social media feeds to check for likes or comments—a digital stamp of approval of who we are. Something as minor as poor audio quality at a speaking event causes us to drown in a flood of self-doubt. We can't stop analyzing our flaws, picking at our scabs, and staring at ourselves in the proverbial mirror. Are we good enough? Successful enough? Kind enough? Talented enough? Even humble enough? We never quite know, and so we're never quite at peace with who we are.

Most of us don't want to appear conceited or arrogant, but we'd love to live our lives with a bit more confidence. We'd prefer to avoid falling flat on our faces; but if we do, wouldn't it be great if we could simply dust ourselves off and keep walking? Instead, we wear ourselves out with endless people-pleasing. Embarrassing moments or inadequacies make us want to crawl in a hole and never come out. Natural shyness spirals into immobilizing fear, and any attention—either positive or negative—can make us want to run to the nearest exit.

But what if, even through mocking or after failure or confession or whatever other unmasking we may face, we could still be okay? What if how we appear and what others think about us didn't have to rock our egos quite so much? What would it be like to feel secure in what God says about us, unswayed by the winds of everyone else's opinion?

THE QUESTION OF GOOD ENOUGH

I read a short poem once that stated the only opinion of you that matters is your own opinion.[2] Who cares what others think, right? That's how our culture answers the problem of insecurity. I get the sentiment, and I agree we can't live our lives solely to placate others. But what happens when we have an exceedingly low opinion of ourselves? What happens when my opinion is that I shouldn't exist any longer? Or what if I go too far the other direction, putting no stock in how my actions or words affect someone else and lean toward narcissism instead? In both of those cases, I—and the world at large—would be better off if I *did* listen to what people around me had to say.

> Beware of anyone who tells you to find yourself by only looking at yourself.

Our insecurity is rooted in the fact that we are looking to ourselves or to others for our source of identity—and no one can give that to us. We keep trying to grasp for it anyway by seeking acceptance or attempting to control outcomes or juggling opinions. When we don't succeed or gain the approval we want, even from ourselves, we feel like failures all the more. Then we drive that animal harder and harder, only to be more exhausted. We find ourselves trapped in an endless feedback loop, a hamster wheel of image management we can't seem to quit.

Friend, beware of anyone who tells you to find yourself by only looking at yourself. Habakkuk, when talking about physical idols, wrote, "What profit is an idol when its maker has shaped it? . . . For its maker trusts in his own creation" (Hab. 2:18). We might not be tempted to craft an image of gold or silver, but we are all too tempted to craft ourselves into our own image. Yet there is no wholeness, no fulfillment, no security in giving up reflecting God's image so we can create and manage our own image instead. Pastor and author Sam Allberry said, "If we look deep inside our hearts, we are not going to find the solution to our angst. We're going to find the cause of it."[3]

We lose ourselves when we lose sight of the One we're supposed to reflect; but when we look at Christ, we can become fully—and securely—ourselves. The message of Scripture is that we find our true knowledge of self, our true security, by first looking to God—and specifically who God is as revealed in Jesus Christ by the Spirit. "I have been crucified with Christ," Paul wrote to the Galatians. "It is no longer I who live, but Christ who lives in me. And the life I now live in the flesh I live by faith in the Son of God, who loved me and gave himself for me" (Gal. 2:20).

The truth about who we are in Christ means that we are free from leaning on ever-changing opinions to determine our value and identity. We're free from needing to evaluate if we're good enough, successful enough, talented enough, even humble enough. "'I am not good enough.' It sounds very modest," wrote Martyn Lloyd-Jones, "but it is the lie of the devil, it is a denial of the faith. You think that you are being humble. But you will never be good enough; nobody has ever been good enough. The essence of the Christian salvation is to say that He is good enough and that I am in Him!"[4]

Our social media habits, our overanalyzing, our relationships, our workaholism, our fear—all those things are an attempt to answer the question of if we're "enough." But the gospel frees us from that uncertainty. Instead of trying to perform to gain approval, we can know Christ has already accepted us, and now we get to live out of that knowledge.

In *The Freedom of Self-Forgetfulness,* Tim Keller wrote:

> Do you realize that it is only in the gospel of Jesus Christ that you get the verdict before the performance? . . . In Christianity, the verdict leads to performance. . . .
>
> You see, the verdict is in. And now I perform on the basis of the verdict. Because He loves me and He accepts me, I do not have to do things just to build up my résumé. I do not have to do things to make me look good. I can do things for the joy of doing them. I can help people to help people—not so I can feel better about myself, not so I can fill up the emptiness. . . .
>
> The only person whose opinion counts looks at me and He finds me more valuable than all the jewels in the earth.[5]

When we are secure in our place in the kingdom of God as His beloved child, we don't need to prove ourselves in front of any judge or jury. The verdict is in, and we get to walk out of the courtroom the moment we are declared righteous through Christ. We are the Lord's. Christ lives in us. Therefore, the question of whether we're good enough isn't even something we have to ask anymore.

FINDING SECURITY IN WHO GOD IS

In Exodus 3 and 4, Moses was minding his own business, hanging out with his father-in-law's sheep in the middle of the wilderness. He had run away from Egypt where he grew up, because Pharaoh had a bone to pick with him about the Egyptian he'd killed. While watching over the sheep near Mount Horeb, an angel appeared and then the voice of God called to him from a burning-but-not-burning-up bush. This was no heat stroke or dehydration talking; Moses spoke to the God of the universe.

The Lord tells Moses that He's seen the suffering and oppression the Israelites have been through. He's going to save them and bring them to a new land, and Moses is going to be a part of it. God says, "Come, I will send you to Pharaoh that you may bring my people, the children of Israel, out of Egypt" (Ex. 3:10).

Even though he grew up in Pharaoh's household, Moses isn't exactly on friendly terms with the ruler of Egypt. He ran for his life because Pharaoh was going to kill him (Ex. 2:15). And God is asking him to go back there?

Moses responds to God with as many excuses as he can come up with. But every time, God has an answer.

"Who am I that I should go to Pharaoh?" (3:11). "I will be with you," God says. Moses then asks what he should tell the Israelites about who's sending him. God replies, "I AM WHO I AM . . . I AM has sent me to you" (3:14). The Lord reassures Moses the people will listen and tells him exactly what to say to both Pharaoh and the elders of Israel.

"But . . . they will not believe me or listen to my voice," Moses argues (4:1). Then God gives him signs of His power, turning Moses' staff into a serpent and then afflicting Moses—and then healing him—from leprosy. *If they don't believe you when they see these signs, I'll turn the Nile into blood.*

But God, I'm not eloquent! Moses pulls out all the stops. He does not want to go back, and can you blame him? He's safe at his father-in-law's place in Midian, and no one seems to want to kill him right now. *God, please don't send me back there!*

"Who has made man's mouth? Who makes him mute, or deaf, or

seeing, or blind? Is it not I, the LORD? Now therefore go, and I will be with your mouth and teach you what you shall speak," God says (4:11–12). Finally, Moses stops hiding behind excuses. He comes right out with it. "Oh, my Lord, please send someone else" (v. 13). Can you hear the exasperation in his voice, the pleading with God to get out of this job? *Please, God, don't make me do it.*

God gets angry at Moses for his excuses and lack of trust, but He agrees to send Moses' brother, Aaron, with him. Aaron is good at speaking, and that'll quell Moses' fear, at least a little. *I'll tell you both what to say and will teach you what to do* (v. 15).

After every excuse, God reminds Moses about who He is and what He will do. *I'll be with you. I AM WHO I AM. I have the power to do miraculous signs and wonders, power that far surpasses Pharaoh's. I am the Creator who made your very mouth. I will do what I promised.* In other words, *Moses, stop looking at yourself and look at who I am. Stop focusing on all your fears and inadequacies—because with Me, those don't even matter. This isn't about you or the bounty on your head or the fact that you can't speak all that well; it's about Me—and I've got this. I've got you.*

God didn't speak to Moses' fear and insecurity by saying, *I know you can do it, Moses!* He didn't even reassure Moses that Pharaoh would be kind or receptive in any way. In fact, God made it clear the king of Egypt wouldn't easily listen (3:19). In other words, neither Moses' opinion of himself nor the opinion of anyone else mattered. God wanted Moses to trust in *Him,* what *He's* capable of, and what *He* could do through—and sometimes in spite of—Moses' insecurity.

When Moses had to take God at His word, that meant he had to return to Egypt and confront Pharaoh. I'm guessing Moses didn't always *feel* comfortable and secure as he made his way through the desert to Egypt. Yet after each step of faith that Moses took, God proved Himself trustworthy and reliable.

There's a very felt risk when we walk out of the proverbial courtroom and give up trying to prove ourselves or manage our image or trust our abilities. It's easy to say, "You're secure in Christ." But it takes an act of faith to put that security to the test. When God calls us to act boldly, do we trust Him to equip us? When God's Word tells us who we are, do we believe Him?

Remember the story of Peter walking on water? Peter sees Jesus out on the sea, and he calls out, "Lord, if it's you . . . tell me to come to you on the water." Jesus tells him to come, so Peter gets out of the boat and walks on the water—until he sees the wind and grows fearful. He cries out to Jesus, and Jesus saves him. That act of getting out of the boat and experiencing Jesus' trustworthiness and reliability strengthened Peter's faith. After they climbed back into the boat and the winds died down, everyone in the boat worshiped Jesus saying, "Truly you are the Son of God" (Matt. 14:33).

The step of faith Peter took forced him to reckon with who Jesus was and whether he could find the very literal security he needed in the midst of wind and waves. It's one thing to say, "Sure, rely on Jesus." It's another thing to be able to say that after you've gotten out of the boat.

LIVING OUT OUR TRUE IDENTITY

Insecurity keeps us timid. It keeps us scared and fearful and unsteady. But knowing who we are in Christ frees us to live with boldness. Moses made up excuses and Peter doubted when the waves came. Yet ultimately, they took risky steps of faith to do what God was calling them to do—even if they were also tentative, excuse-laden, fear-filled steps. It took an immense amount of courage (some might even say reckless-ness) for Moses to go back to Egypt and for Peter to climb out of that boat. Yet they did, and God held them secure.

We can have that same kind of faith, daily putting one foot in front of the other as we trust God with our lives, vocations, and relationships. We can talk to a crowd, even while our hands shake and the sweat smudges our notecards. We can open our home to people who are different than us, start a new job, call out injustice, speak truth to power, or refuse to engage in unethical or unkind behavior in our workplaces without fearing the possible repercussions. We can also confess our sin to others and seek forgiveness. Admitting our own mistakes can be uncomfortable, especially when we're unsure how someone will react. But knowing we're not on trial anymore enables us to do what God asks—even if it hurts, even if it costs us our reputations or more.

When we let go of insecurity, we're also free to take both compliments and criticism. I remember as a kid my mom teaching me how to receive a compliment. Even now, I can see my six-year-old self hiding behind her legs and clinging to the back of her dress in the hallway at church. Someone would say something like, "Great job in the kids' choir!" or "I like your braids!" My mom would coax me to say thank you, but I only wanted to run behind the brooms inside the nearest supply closet. Part of my response stemmed from my naturally shy personality, but I also did not know how to receive kind words from someone without my insides squirming. I felt exposed by their words, as if under the spotlight. I'd rather tiptoe away from the attention and avoid the risk of being seen at all.

Sometimes applause can make us feel uncomfortable. Other times, critique knocks the emotional wind out of us for a week. We can inhale compliments like a glutton at a feast rather than receiving them with gratitude and humility. Or we get overly defensive when someone points out a mistake or misstep. But when our eyes are more focused on reflecting the image of God than maintaining our own, we can receive compliments and honor with gratitude. We can consider criticism, letting untrue words slide off our back and allowing true ones to shape us for the better. Neither compliments nor critiques rock the person whose identity is secure.[6]

Finding our security in Christ also frees us to serve others. An insecure person would never want to be seen doing humble tasks or defaulting to someone they see as "below" them. But Jesus never cared if He looked good in the eyes of others. He never put His reputation above His calling. He never said He couldn't serve because doing so was beneath Him. As God in the form of man, it was *all* beneath Him. The entire incarnation was an act of service. Paul wrote in Philippians:

> Though he was in the form of God, did not count equality with God a thing to be grasped, but emptied himself, by taking the form of a servant, being born in the likeness of men. And being found in human form, he humbled himself by becoming obedient to the point of death, even death on a cross. (Phil. 2:6–8)

Jesus stooped to our level to come to earth as a human —and He didn't stop there. He ate with tax collectors, hung out with sinners, faced the wrath of the Pharisees, and washed the dirty feet of the disciples, including the one who would soon betray Him. Not once did He fear what others thought of Him or attempt to manage His image. *And He was the very Son of God!* How much more should we humbly serve others, no matter what the people around us think?

Letting go of insecurity also means we are free to rest. When we're insecure, we can be tempted to respond "yes" to every request, fearing what someone might think if we decline. So many of us avoid physical rest because our identity is bound up in our productivity. We'd rather heap on the burden of overwork than risk being perceived as an unhelpful or inattentive person. Or we can all too easily forget to take care of ourselves because we're consumed with answering to others.

But when we believe we belong to God, we take care of what is God's. *That includes us.* The kingdom will not fall apart if we sit down and take a breath. But we can be tempted to believe God's relying on us to get all the work done. That's disordered thinking. We're expecting ourselves to do what only God can instead of recognizing that we are fully reliant on Him. He chooses to use us, thank God, but He doesn't need us to do work He's never given us to do. As one author said, "Grace enables quality, hard work. Grace does not inspire fruitless overwork."[7]

OUR UNADORNED SELF

Henri Nouwen once told a story about leaving the academic world to live in a community of people with intellectual disabilities. He wrote:

The first thing that struck me when I came to live [in that community] was that their liking or disliking of me had absolutely nothing to do with any of the many useful things I had done until then. Since nobody could read my books, the books could not impress anyone, and since most of them never went to school, my twenty years at Notre Dame, Yale, and Harvard did not provide a significant introduction. . . .

Not being able to use any of the skills that had proved so practical in the past was a real source of anxiety. I was suddenly faced with my naked self, open for affirmations and rejections, hugs and punches, smiles and tears, all dependent simply on how I was perceived at the moment. In a way, it seemed as though I was starting my life all over again. Relationships, connections, reputations could no longer be counted on.

This experience was and, in many ways, is still the most important experience of my new life, because it forced me to rediscover my true identity. These broken, wounded, and completely unpretentious people forced me to let go of my relevant self—the self that can do things, show things, prove things, build things—and forced me to reclaim that unadorned self in which I am completely vulnerable, open to receive and give love regardless of any accomplishments.[8]

What would it be like to experience that bareness, that exposure, that inability to hide behind a thick blanket of accomplishments or usefulness, or whatever it is we tend to clothe ourselves with, and be totally unashamed? What would it look like to stand before our friends and family and the world and God with our "unadorned self" and know that no matter our scars and scrapes, our failures or even our fortunes, we are okay?

That's the kind of freedom we can have when we know who we are in Christ. That's the kind of rest we experience when we're not overanalyzing opinions or trying to prove ourselves.

I've tried to get approval from others through overwork or performing. I've felt anxiety and fear because I was uncertain how others perceived me. But I've also experienced the freedom of being able to walk out of a room knowing, no matter what happened, no matter what others thought, no matter how I need to do things better next time, I am okay. I can show my "unadorned self" and know that I am enough—not because of anything I did, but because of what God says about me and who Christ is in me.

It can feel impossible to let go of insecurity when there are people in your life who make you feel small. It's hard to believe what God says about you if you already think little of yourself. But we have to learn to step away from the noise and let God's voice be the loudest in the room. We have to let His words pour over our soul. And when we listen to what He says and trust He's telling us the truth, what we think will begin to align with what He thinks. We'll begin to view ourselves and others the way He views us and find the rest and security we need.

REFLECT

1. When was a time that you felt insecure? What truth from Scripture helps to steady you?

2. What's something you use to answer the question of whether you're enough? Do you have a tendency to find your "enoughness" on social media? Do you depend too much on validation from your boss or your friends or your family? Do you try to find approval through obsessively managing your appearance or your home?

3. When we're secure in who we are in Christ, we can be bold, take compliments and criticism, serve others, and rest. Which one of those four categories do you struggle with most? How can you take a tangible step of faith this week to do that particular thing? For example, maybe you struggle with resting. What would it look like for you to rest in the next few days?

Chapter 7

COMPARISON

Holding Out for Something Better

Oh, taste and see that the LORD is good! Blessed is the man who takes refuge in him! Oh, fear the LORD, you his saints, for those who fear him have no lack! The young lions suffer want and hunger; but those who seek the LORD lack no good thing.

• PSALM 34:8–10

Wouldn't you like to be the skater who wins the silver, and yet is thrilled about those three triple jumps that the gold medal winner did? To love it the way you love a sunrise? Just to love the fact that it was done? For it not to matter whether it was their success or your success. Not to care if they did it or you did it. You are as happy that they did it as if you had done it yourself—because you are just so happy to see it.

• TIMOTHY KELLER

A STACK OF COMMENTARIES and articles sat on the corner of my desk. Fluorescent pink sticky notes bookmarked important pages. Rough drafts marked up in red filled my computer and printed copies spilled onto the floor in my office. I spent hours upon hours upon hours researching and writing for what I hoped and prayed would be a book. I poured a good part of a year into that proposal. A few people I'd pitched the idea to gave me positive feedback, including a literary agent. The project seemed to be moving forward, and I was bound and determined to make it come to fruition.

Eventually, though, those talks with that agent stopped, my emails went unanswered. The book proposal sat in the abyss of a few others' email inboxes (or junk folders). The entire process of researching, writing, and pitching my book came to a screeching halt, and discouragement started to build. Was I supposed to give up? Did I need to press forward, even though it seemed like I kept hitting a wall? I felt like a tired old car that had sputtered and stalled on the side of the road, not going anywhere. Then, to add a little salt to my wounded ego, it seemed like every time I scrolled my Instagram feed, someone else was celebrating the release of a book *on the exact same topic.*

When I saw one of those announcements, I muttered like a preschooler who doesn't want to share, "But that's *my* book!" It seemed like everyone else was effortlessly landing book deals as they wrote and spoke about what I wanted to be the one to say. *No fair!*

When I'd see their posts, envy and bitterness rose in my chest. I'm ashamed to admit I found myself wanting to hit "unfollow" instead of celebrating their work or sharing their words. I started to fixate on growing my social media and email list numbers just so I could get a book deal as quickly as possible—because what if yet another person gets to that elusive finish line first?

My work that started out with the goal of showcasing the goodness of God became tainted by my desire to get ahead—or at least catch up. Without realizing it at first, my book became about me and what I had to say, and when my project didn't happen, that failure—and others' successes—felt deeply personal. My thoughts swung from one extreme to the other. Sometimes I complained, "Why isn't my book getting published? It's better!" Other times I felt like shouting, "My writing is terrible. They already wrote what I wanted to write. Why should I even bother?"

One afternoon, as I wallowed in my own dejection and saw yet another person had released a book on "my" topic, a question came to mind: *Is the most important thing that the message gets out or that I get to be the one to say it?* The question seemed to come out of nowhere, and I couldn't shake the conviction from the Holy Spirit that came with it. What if I could set my pride aside and learn from these other writers? What if God had reasons for the pause in this project, and I'm stomping my feet in anger at Him instead of trusting His timing? What if, instead of comparing myself to others around me, I celebrated them?

THE PROBLEMS COMPARISON BREEDS

I grew up as the youngest of six kids, and my mom regularly cooked delicious homemade meals. Because there were a lot of us and the food tasted so good, we all tended to eat *very* quickly. I joke that in my family, if you don't eat fast, you don't eat. My husband learned that lesson early in our marriage on a family vacation. He had spent time frying up bacon for over twenty people for BLT sandwiches, but when he finally went to assemble his own sandwich, he found only a few drippings of grease left on the serving plate. He didn't grab what he needed fast enough and was left empty-handed.

We sometimes worry we'll be stuck in that same kind of situation, don't we! We've seen how quickly good things run out, and we start to fear there won't be anything left for us. So, we hoard or hurry, scarfing down what we can while we can, all while glancing through the corner of our eye at what the person next to us has. We want to make sure we didn't miss anything or we won't be left wanting or everyone's portions are fair.

We also want to be assured that we'll measure up to others. I've run a handful of road races over the years, and I know I'll never be in the front of the pack. But more than once, I've rallied my legs to move faster by whispering to myself, "Just don't come in last!" Being last would just be too embarrassing. I do the same thing in the rest of my life. I live in a rush, striving and toiling in a vain attempt to keep up with everyone else only to find that, as author Alan Fadling wrote, "My hurry is what often makes the yoke of life and ministry heavier than Jesus means it to be."[1]

We compare ourselves to others all the time. We fight for positions of honor or power. We see the well-behaved kids, the steady job, the pristine decor, or the exceptional talent and grow bitter about the hand we've been dealt. We compare our bodies and belongings to our neighbor's or the stranger's on the internet. We compare our accomplishments to what others have done, our educational choices, the fullness of our calendars, the stability of our family. *How is she able to do all of that? I can barely hold it together.* We can compare ourselves to ourselves, longing for what we used to be or where we thought we'd be by now. We compare our suffering and struggles, playing a sort of twisted game of "Whose life is harder?" And we even compare our sins, judging others who are "worse" and carrying shame when that's us.

Comparison wreaks havoc on our lives. It breeds envy, overwork, bitterness, striving, and discontent in our own hearts. It tears down our relationships with others. But we don't have to give in to the mindset that we're all competing against each other, and we don't have to fear we'll be left holding an empty plate with only a few streaks of bacon grease. Because God is generous, compassionate, and fully self-sufficient. He is never in a rush, and He's never going to run out of resources. His kingdom doesn't measure people the same way we do, and He promises He won't withhold good from those who walk with Him (Ps. 84:11). If only we can have the patience to wait for the good He wants to give us and trust His definition of good is far better than our own.

I did not wait well when every door slammed shut on the project I was passionate about. But as it turns out, God's timing really was better. After submitting the proposal for that book project, I went through the dark season of depression and anxiety I talk about in this book. Truthfully, I could not have written my original book during that season. I also recently looked back at that first proposal, and as I read it, I couldn't help but cringe at the style of my writing and the immaturity of my content. I was not ready, and God knew it.

A COMPASSIONATE AND GENEROUS MASTER

There's a story in Matthew 20 about a vineyard owner and the workers he hires.[2] I still recoil sometimes when I read it, because in my view, the way things pan out seems so unfair. But God's kingdom doesn't work the way mine does.

Jesus tells His listeners the kingdom of heaven is like a master of a vineyard who heads out to the marketplace to find workers. There, potential employees gather, waiting to see if anyone will hire them.[3] The master shows up, offers a day's wage (one denarius), and heads back with his new employees to the vineyard. A few hours later, he comes back to the marketplace to hire more workers who continue to stand waiting and ready. The day is young, and if they can get hired now, they can still earn a decent wage—although the owner makes no mention of how much he'll pay, just that the wage will be fair (Matt. 20:4). He hires a few, and they set off to work.

Then the vineyard owner goes to the marketplace again. And again. And again. Each time, he finds people eager for work. Each time, they're ready and willing—and growing increasingly more desperate—to get hired so they can bring some pay home to their families. Each time, the group that's left gets a little more dejected, a little more humiliated they haven't been hired, a little more fearful the bellies of their children will growl louder.

Five times in all, the owner of the vineyard returns to the marketplace to hire workers. Only the group hired first thing in the morning is under a contract for a specific amount. When the day is done, the ragtag group hired at the very end of the day—those who had stood watching others get picked first—receives the same pay as everyone else. A denarius—a full day's wage. The group who worked from sunup watches this transaction eagerly at first. *Wow! If he paid those guys for only an hour or two, think how much more we'll get paid!* But each worker receives the same amount, whether they worked one hour or twelve.

The first group is not having it. "These last worked only one hour, and you have made them equal to us who have borne the burden of the day and the scorching heat" (Matt. 20:12). *It's not fair! We've been working longer and harder—and we get the same?*[4]

The owner replies, "Friend, I am doing you no wrong. Did you not agree with me for a denarius? Take what belongs to you and go. I choose to give to this last worker as I give to you. Am I not allowed to do what I choose with what belongs to me? Or do you begrudge my generosity?" (vv. 13–15).

Jesus doesn't tell us what their response was. Did they stomp away in anger while stuffing their pay in their pockets? That's probably what I would have done. I remember one time in fourth grade working for days—weeks—on a diorama for social studies class only to find out the teacher gave pretty much everyone who turned in something, *anything*, an A. I'm still a little annoyed about it.

But Jesus' point isn't that we should always pay everyone the same or that we should give everyone an A regardless of how much work they do. He's telling this story to illustrate a truth about the kingdom of God.

No one in this story was underpaid. The first group hired received their agreed-upon wages, and the rest received far more than they deserved. After all, why did the master go out to the marketplace *five separate times?* Wouldn't he have known how many workers he needed? While it's possible he underestimated the first time and needed to go back again, he likely went back again and again because he was looking to see who else needed work. Who's left in the marketplace still trying to bring home a few bucks with which they can try to feed their families? It's as if he thought, *The day is almost done, but I wonder if anyone is still there. I wonder who's still waiting and in need.* The master could have sent his manager to find workers, but the master himself returns—and not because he's a poor judge of his labor needs. The master returns because he is compassionate, kind, and generous.

The character of the master makes some of us, like the first group of laborers, mad. Author and New Testament lecturer Kenneth Bailey explains:

> The story focuses on an equation filled with amazing grace, which is resented by those who feel that they have earned their way to more. . . . To their market-oriented minds, their worth as human beings is directly related to how much they are paid. Grace is not only amazing, it is also—for certain types— *infuriating.*[5]

In the kingdom of God, the first shall be last and the last shall be first, Jesus tells His listeners (twice).[6] Maybe He's even saying this in response to Peter, who asked just prior to this parable, "See, we have left everything and followed you. What then will *we* have?" (Matt. 19:27).

We want to get our fair share, don't we? We want to be rewarded for who we are and what we've done. Others of us are like the men hired at the last hour of the day, dejected, penniless, and desperate for someone to give us a chance. Then the master of the vineyard comes and shows us abundant grace no matter what we bring to the table.

In the kingdom of heaven, God can do what He wants with what He has. He can show mercy, He can show compassion, He can lavish grace on the thief on the cross or to the disciples who followed Him from the beginning. For those listening, this parable would have spoken directly against the idea that those who appeared "righteous" like the Pharisees would be the ones to receive the greatest share of God's favor in the kingdom. But God so loved the *whole* world—sinner and righteous, successful and struggling.

This is the way the kingdom works. This is who our God is— generous and compassionate. He's also the one in charge, the one with the prerogative to divvy up His gifts the way He wants. As Jackie Hill Perry said, "The holy, holy, holy God owes us nothing, but His compassion is what He's given us anyway."[7]

According to scholar Craig Blomberg, Matthew 20:15, the verse where the master asks, "Do you begrudge my generosity?" can be more literally translated, "Is your eye evil because I am good?"[8] When God gives to someone else—whether it's salvation or success or material wealth or anything else—do we give in to evil because He's good? Does His generosity make us jealous, or does it cause us to celebrate?

What we do and have are for His glory and honor. But when we leave our penchant for comparison unchecked, it can lead to envy and frustration. The laborers in the vineyard begrudged what the others had received. They distrusted the Giver when they could have been reveling in the goodness of God.

How much more joy would the first group have experienced if, instead of brooding in anger, they celebrated with those who were given far more than they deserved? If we compare at all, let us compare in order to rejoice in God's lavishness, in the measure of grace someone else receives.

If we know God is generous and compassionate, we can trust Him with what we have *and* what others have. We can steward well what God has given us, rejoicing in the fact that every good gift comes from Him—even if we're not the one to receive it.

COMPARING OUR SUFFERING

"I got no sleep last night," a friend complains. "I hear you—I haven't slept in a week," we respond. It's a silly example, but we've all done this—and have had it done to us. Comparison isn't limited to our *stuff* like our successes, our material possessions, our relationships, our bodies. We also compare our struggles and our suffering. We do this weird thing where we try to one-up each other by how hard our lives are.

We also try to compartmentalize or justify instead of offering empathy. As a person or community grieves, we respond with, "Well, what about this other tragedy?" It's like we're lining up all kinds of suffering next to each other to see who deserves our compassion.

Other times, we minimize our own pain because we know it's not as bad as what a friend is going through. "I can still function most days," I often said to myself when trying to gauge my level of depression. "So-and-so has it so much worse." While that may have been true, for too long I used the fact that someone else had it worse than I did as a reason to not get the help I needed. We shove our own grief into a corner, because shouldn't we just be grateful? When we do this, we end up alone and stuck in our pain instead of finding the healing and help we need.

There is no value in deeming one set of tears more valid than another. Please don't hear me wrong—yes, we do need to keep various kinds of suffering in perspective. A broken leg is not as bad as the death of a loved one. We know this. But sometimes, in the name of having perspective, we sweep very real pain under the rug, either others' or our own. We start to believe one set of struggles isn't worth grieving or sharing at all, and we all end up in our own corners, suffering alone.

We have a God who sees even when a sparrow falls. He doesn't turn His back on our seemingly small suffering, and He also knows the greatest griefs one can endure. No amount of suffering is too small or too great for Him to hold, no amount of heartache disqualified from His compassion. Isaiah 53:4 says that the Messiah bore our griefs and carried our sorrows. There was no exception, no time He said, "Oh, except that grief and that sorrow." He carried it *all* to the cross.

Comparison hamstrings compassion. We need to ask God for wisdom and practice discernment to know when and how to share our tears and respond to others'. It can come off as callous or tone-deaf if we try to lament our daily struggles with someone grieving horrendous tragedy. But one-upping each other, minimizing pain, or offering "whataboutisms" is not what we are called to do. Instead, as Paul wrote, "Rejoice with those who rejoice, weep with those who weep" (Rom. 12:15).

AT LEAST I'M NOT LIKE *THAT* PERSON

There were two men, Jesus told His listeners.[9] A Pharisee and a tax collector. They both go up to the temple. The Pharisee stands far away, likely to avoid touching someone like the tax collector who he considered to be unclean. He prays, *Thank You, Lord, that I'm not like murderers or extortioners or even like this tax collector over here. I fast and tithe even beyond what's required by the law.*

Among those who had gathered to hear from Jesus were those who "trusted in themselves" and "treated others with contempt" (Luke 18:9). Maybe some of the disciples thought this way, and maybe a few Pharisees stood within earshot. Jesus' listeners would likely have been impressed by the fictional Pharisee. "The first hearers of this parable would not think of the Pharisee as boastful, but rather as grateful to God for his piety,"[10] remarked biblical scholar Craig Keener. They're nodding along, amazed at how this man of God didn't just fast once a year, as the law required, or even before and after each of the three major feasts, like many Pharisees did. This guy fasts *every single week*. Not only that, but instead of tithing grain, oil, and wine, as the law required, he tithes on "all that I get" (Luke 18:12).[11]

Jesus then contrasts the Pharisee with the description of the tax collector, a hated figure who worked for the Roman Empire and often cheated his Jewish neighbors in the process. The tax collector hangs his head and "beats his breast." He pounds on his chest, so deeply distraught over his own sin and cries out to God for mercy. Kenneth Bailey noted that his plea for mercy is literally a plea for God to "make an atonement."[12] He begs God not merely for leniency, but for forgiveness.

Maybe Jesus pauses here as He tells the story. I imagine Him letting His listeners think for a minute, giving them space to reflect on their own judgments about the two men. *Pharisee: good. Tax collector: bad.* Then Jesus turns every expectation upside down and says of the tax collector, "I tell you, this man went down to his house justified, rather than the other. For everyone who exalts himself will be humbled, but the one who humbles himself will be exalted" (Luke 18:14).

His listeners would have been shocked at how this story ended. The type of person they hated, the person who stole from his Jewish friends and family, the person who worked for the enemy, went home from the temple justified? Not the supposedly holy, law-abiding man who went above and beyond what he was required to do? *Really, Jesus?*

The problem with the Pharisee is that he compared himself to others instead of to God.[13] We do this too. Maybe we don't stand in our churches offering prayers that are (not so) thinly veiled compliments of our own holiness like he did. But we still compare our sin to others.

> **Grace is not given based on the merits of the recipient but because of the character of the Giver.**

"At least I'm not like *that person*," we mutter. Even if we've never said those words out loud, we've all thought it. We've all watched someone else fail or fall and whispered to ourselves how we would never do *that*.

We shake our heads with disdain. *How could they have ever done or said or believed something so terrible or untrue?*

But we are all prone to wander. We are all in desperate need of the grace of God, grace He offers freely and generously. That truth doesn't mean we take sin lightly. Quite the contrary—we should mourn and weep over how we've broken God's law and therefore our relationship with Him. It's also true that some of the ways we sin cause more damage than others, so yes, in that sense some sins are "worse." But the moment we start to think we need God's grace less than the person next to us is the moment we've lost sight of God's holiness and our *own* sin. For "God opposes the proud but gives grace to the humble" (James 4:6).

Comparing our sin sets us up for either self-righteousness or self-condemnation. We either take on the role of the Pharisee in Luke 18, believing we have earned God's grace; or we believe we're too far gone, our sins too big for that grace ever to reach us. But grace is not given based on the merits of the recipient but because of the character of the Giver. Even if we are the one at our lowest, the one standing far off begging God for forgiveness, even then, we can trust there's no depth of sin His grace cannot reach (Rom. 5:20). Like the tax collector, like the Pharisee, we all need grace. Thanks be to God that He freely gives it.

THE GREATER REWARD IS COMING

When I was working on that very first book proposal (which is still collecting digital dust on my computer), so much of my motivation came from a fear of slipping into the back of the pack, a fear of not measuring up. If I fell behind everyone else, what they were doing and accomplishing, would there be any room left for me? But a shift began to take place in my soul. Through the conviction of the Holy Spirit, I began to see how exhausted I'd become by elbowing my way forward and sizing myself up against the person next to me.

I started sharing others' work and celebrating their accomplishments.

I joined book launch teams and wrote rave reviews for writing I loved, even when I didn't always feel like doing that. There were days I read someone else's books or articles and wished they were mine. Yet God was untangling me daily from the web of comparison. And you know what? Celebrating others is way more fun than comparing myself to them. Cultivating community offers more joy than pitting myself against others ever can. Practicing compassion, while not always easy, is far more God-honoring than building resentment.

In Philippians 3, Paul wrote, "But one thing I do: forgetting what lies behind and straining forward to what lies ahead, I press on toward the goal for the prize of the upward call of God in Christ Jesus" (vv. 13–14). Being stuck in comparison means we've lost sight of what's ahead. We've turned our gaze to the right or left, focusing on how our stuff or our suffering or our sin measures up to the person next to us. We want our desires and dreams in this life more than what God has to offer in the next. Often we're like the disciples who, during their last meal with Jesus before He died for them and for us, got in an argument over who was the greatest. *You really want to know who is the greatest? The one who serves,* Jesus tells them.[14]

The one who serves believes the reward to come is better than anything life offers now. As believers, we are not all fighting for a lone trophy, as if there's only one prize God is giving out. We're living as new creations, working to receive the "crown of life" (James 1:12). We're following in the footsteps of Moses who "considered the reproach of Christ greater wealth than the treasures of Egypt, for he was looking to the reward" (Heb. 11:26). We're holding out for "something better" that God promises instead of clamoring for immediate honor (v. 40).

We don't have to spend our days calculating where we stand or how we measure up to others around us. Instead, we fix our eyes on our generous, compassionate, gracious God, faithfully marching forward until we hear the only words that will matter in the end:

"Well done, good and faithful servant" (Matt. 25:23).

REFLECT

1. In what ways do you struggle with comparison? Do you compare what you have? Do you tend to compare suffering or struggle with comparing your sin?

2. When you read the parable of the master of the vineyard, what's your knee-jerk reaction to the way he paid his workers? Do you find yourself rejoicing over his generosity or lamenting the seeming unfairness of it?

3. What would it look like for you this week to practice celebrating someone else rather than comparing yourself to them?

Chapter 8

PERFECTIONISM

Grace for What Life Is

*Count it all joy, my brothers, when you meet trials of various
kinds, for you know that the testing of your faith produces
steadfastness. And let steadfastness have its full effect, that you
may be perfect and complete, lacking in nothing.*

> • JAMES 1:2–4

*If we let him . . . He will make the feeblest and filthiest of us into a
god or goddess, a dazzling, radiant, immortal creature, pulsating
all through with such energy and joy and wisdom and love as
we cannot now imagine, a bright stainless mirror which reflects
back to God perfectly (though, of course, on a smaller scale) His
own boundless power and delight and goodness. The process will
be long and in parts very painful, but that is what we are in for.
Nothing less. He meant what he said.*

> • C. S. LEWIS

THERE'S A BLANKET THROWN over a chair, papers strewn next to my computer, dishes on the counter. LEGO block "landmines" cover the floors throughout my home. The laundry isn't folded, all the carpets need to be replaced, and nail holes punctuate several walls thanks to my tendency to eyeball it when hanging frames. One of these days, I'll fill them in with the container of spackle I bought over two years ago.

I like my house clean and neat. I enjoy a well-designed home and beautiful decor. But those things are not my forte, nor my passion. Especially in this stage of life with young kids, I've loosened the reins on perfectionism at home and embraced a "good enough" standard. In many ways, I've gone further and exchanged a "good enough" attitude for an "ehhh, it'll be fine" mentality.

My dear, sweet husband on the other hand . . . let's just say he's the one who does anything requiring exacting skill and a careful eye. We have a gallery wall in our family room, each image hung perfectly by him. He often walks by those pictures and straightens them just so, ensuring every edge lines up parallel to the edge of the next. What do I do? I stealthily walk past and push down the edge of a few frames to skew the alignment of the gallery wall. It's just because I love him— and I like to drive him a little crazy teasing him about his perfectionist tendencies.

I struggled with perfectionism in high school, overcommitting, pushing myself too hard, and feeling like a failure when I didn't get the results I wanted. I had so many early morning practices, rehearsals, or meetings that I often had to trek down to the maintenance office to find someone to unlock the building for me. Even the teachers hadn't arrived yet. By the end of my junior year, I started to unravel. I fell asleep at the dinner table one night while my dad prayed over our food. I once ran out of gas on my way to a band rehearsal, not because I was unaware the gas light was on in my car, but because I simply did not have time to stop at a gas station. By senior year, I spent an evening in my room lamenting about how I wanted to quit every single activity because I had nothing left to give. I didn't quit everything, thankfully, and I had people in my life who listened and then helped me navigate the rest of that year with a little more realism and grace than I could muster up for myself. But I clearly remember thinking that night, "I never want to feel this run-down again."

When I went away for college, it felt like I could start with a fresh slate and an empty calendar. That calendar filled up quickly, but for the first time, I practiced saying no to extra commitments. I could more quickly notice warning signs like sleeplessness, anxiousness, and being hyper-focused on achievement, and when I noticed myself wearing down, I'd adjust accordingly. I started to see the value of going deep instead of spreading myself thin. Unlike when I was in high school, I finally began to believe that running myself ragged with achievement wasn't a requirement for living.

Years later, as our home has filled up with more kids and more chaos, I figured any remaining perfectionist tendencies got booted out the door by default. I simply haven't had the physical space in my home or mental space in my brain to strive for the perfect home or the perfect body or the perfect parenting plan. I thought I'd kicked my perfectionism habit long ago.

But hi. I'm Sarah. And I'm still a perfectionist.

WHEN THINGS GO AWRY

My perfectionism may not show up in the tidiness of my kitchen or the decor on my walls, but it still lurks beneath the surface of my heart and mind. Perfectionism is about control—and I like control. Perfectionists often want to make sure we appear put together. We want our kids to stay well behaved, and we'd like our relationships or reputation to align perfectly with our own ideals. We want to be in control of what others think or what happens in a given circumstance.

I remember getting so angry once when one of my kids threw a tantrum in the (very quiet) library. On the drive home, after I clenched my teeth and raised my voice far too loudly, I realized so much of that anger came from my fear of what others may have thought about me as a mom. We want to avoid negative thoughts from others. We want to avoid feeling bad about ourselves. And why wouldn't we? No one wants to feel judged or shamed, and it's right to not want to feel that way. But we can go too far in an attempt to avoid that judgment or shame by striving for perfection, or the closest version of perfection possible.

Perfectionists can also be averse to taking certain risks. Risk requires us to give up control to some degree. If something is a risk, that means failure is possible. Some of us (raising my hand again) don't even want to start a project or an endeavor because we wonder, What if it doesn't turn out? There are too many unknowns, too much we can't control. We fear failure and fear mistakes to the point where we feel paralyzed.

Perfectionism is different than striving for excellence, working hard, and seeking to improve. It's an unhealthy fixation and reliance on a perfect state of being or set of circumstances in order for things to be what you want them to be. Perfectionists try to live up to (often impossible) ideals, or they expect others to live up to those ideals too. That pursuit can lead to consequences like burnout, overwork, and— like I've seen in my own life—anger.

When things go awry, our response can reveal our perfectionism. While I get plenty frustrated when my floors reach a certain level of messy and—let's be honest—sticky, I don't care all that much about keeping my house perfect. But when my kids act out in public? Or when my carefully curated calendar gets messed up because of sickness or cancellations? Or when I've spent all day chopping and mixing and sautéing ingredients for a meal that ends up sloppy or burned? My perfectionism becomes painfully clear.

Perfectionism can show up in much deeper ways too. Maybe we envisioned a certain kind of life for ourselves or our family, but our life isn't panning out the way we'd hoped. It's okay—and even good—to grieve the loss of what we wanted or mourn fractured relationships. But what do we do after that? What is our response to God and others when our relationships or careers or lives in general don't live up to our original ideal?

The church, too, has a history of perfectionism. We call it legalism. We can be more concerned about following rules and looking like a good Christian than becoming more like Christ. Perfectionism turns our faith into a performance and prevents us from receiving God's grace—and then extending that grace to ourselves and others.

Thankfully, there's a way to live that doesn't require us to live up to the arbitrary standards we or society set. We don't have to maintain a perfect house or create the perfect family. We don't need to perform in front of others or fear the loss of control. We don't have to despair when our life starts to crack (or shatter entirely) and nothing looks the way we had pictured. We don't have to hold on to perfectionism at all because there's a better way. It's working, instead, toward biblical *perfection.*

HOW TO BE PERFECT

In Matthew 5, a crowd gathers to listen to Jesus, the new itinerant preacher they keep hearing about. The people press in closer, so Jesus goes up on the mountain and sits down, and the disciples gather around Him. He teaches about who is truly "blessed" and what it means to be salt and light. Then, almost like He's reading the minds of His skeptics, He says He hasn't come to get rid of the Law and the Prophets but to fulfill them (v. 17). *Don't soften these commandments,* Jesus says.[1] *Do them. Follow the commands—in fact, go further than what the law says.*

He gives examples of what the law required and how we should go beyond those requirements, pursuing an even greater righteousness that exceeds what the Pharisees and scribes do (Matt. 5:20). *The law says don't murder? Well, I say don't even attack someone with your words. The law says don't commit adultery? I say don't even look at someone with a hint of lust. You know you're supposed to love your neighbor? Don't stop there. Love even your enemies, and pray for those who persecute you (even the Romans!).*[2] Then Jesus sums it all up by saying this: "You therefore must be perfect, as your heavenly Father is perfect" (Matt. 5:48).

Perfect? It's hard enough to live out the letter of the law. Yet Jesus called His followers to do even more. The Greek word for "perfect" here is *teleios,*[3] and its meaning has to do with completeness, wholeness, full maturity. Jesus' point isn't about being a perfectionist. The scribes and Pharisees were already there, demanding full compliance with the law of Moses. Jesus, though, wanted His followers to not just obey the rules but to reflect the heart of the Father.

Perfectionism tries to live up to our human norms and expectations. In their perfectionist attempts to follow it, the Pharisees often twisted the God-given law to reflect their own standards. But as believers, God calls us to live His way because it brings Him glory, it's the only real path to joy, and it has the power to change the world. We're to "exhibit the family likeness," as theologian John Stott put it.[4] "Our Christian calling is to imitate not the world, but the Father. And it is by this imitation of him that the Christian counter-culture becomes visible."[5]

Later in His ministry, Jesus meets a young man, probably between the ages of twenty and forty. He is wealthy and spiritually enthusiastic— like the first-century version of the kid in the front row of a classroom waving his hand in the air to be called on. He's likely a synagogue leader, but not one of those religious elite trying to trick Jesus.[6] He seems sincere as he approaches the Teacher. "Teacher, what good deed must I do to have eternal life?"

"Keep the commandments," Jesus tells him.

"Which ones?"

Maybe the man is asking which ones are the most important. Maybe he's double-checking to see if he passes the test for eternal life. Jesus answers in an unsurprising way, recounting several of the commandments—notably the ones that require a certain kind of outward behavior like not stealing or committing adultery.

Is that it? the man seems to say. *There must be something more.* He wants to do his best. He wants eternal life. But he also seems to know something is missing.

"Jesus said to him, 'If you would be *perfect*, go, sell what you possess and give to the poor, and you will have treasure in heaven; and come, follow me'" (Matt. 19:21).

The man's face falls. He hangs his head and turns to walk away. He's done everything right, he thought. But now Jesus points out that his lifelong pursuit of perfectionism was not enough. His good standing before the community is not enough. His wealth is not enough—in fact, in his case, it's holding him back. He's still incomplete and immature in his faith. His heart and mind are divided; he's not *teleios*.

It would have been a common belief in Jewish minds at that time that the man's wealth was a result of God's favor and a reward for his faithfulness. He was an upstanding Jew, well-respected with deep pockets and seemingly on God's good side. But that day, Jesus confronted him with the one snare holding him back from being truly perfect, the trap that kept him from being a part of the kingdom. For this man, that snare was his possessions. Jesus called the man to a life of dependence, but the man wanted control. His desire for control led to his being controlled by what he had. His wealth allowed him to feel self-sufficient. His faithfulness to the law made him feel like maybe he'd earned his way into God's good graces.

"The young man's request for some 'good thing' to do has brought him face to face with goodness at a level which will prove too high for him," wrote one commentator.[7] As Jesus pointed out in the Sermon on the Mount, merely following the letter of the law was inadequate. By calling the man to sell, give, come, and follow, Jesus reveals to the man that his heart was not wholeheartedly on board with what the kingdom life required. Jesus wants the man to be dependent entirely on Him for

> Letting go of perfectionism means we let go of our tight grip on whatever we hold most dear and surrender it to God instead.

his everyday living now and the life to come. "The essence of Jesus' demand is not disinvestment but discipleship."[8]

We are always in need of Jesus, and God's grace is never earned. It's freely given, but sometimes to accept it, we have to open our hands and let go of what we've clutched for so long. Perfectionism—the careful curation of his life to reach the outcome he wanted—shut this man down to receiving the good God had for him.

The solution then, according to Jesus, is surrender.

Letting go of perfectionism means we let go of our tight grip on whatever we hold most dear and surrender it to God instead. Maybe it's our material wealth. But maybe it's something else—a picture-perfect family life, our health, our careers. It's not that having money in our bank accounts or establishing a career or growing a family is bad; those can all be gifts from God. But gifts that control us are idols, and idols have no place in a kingdom already radiating with God's glory.

We cannot become mature without surrender. As we surrender all we do and have to Jesus, God shapes and molds us to a mature person more fully ourselves and more clearly reflecting Christ. We won't be perfect this side of the new creation, but as N. T. Wright urges, "We should live in the present as people who are to be made complete in the future."[9] Holding on to that promise, not perfectionism, is the goal of the Christian.

PERFECTED THROUGH SUFFERING

Surrender means we give up our desire for control and stop fighting God's work in our lives. The hard reality, though, is that God often works in our lives through suffering. Perfectionism tries to avoid suffering by doubling down on control, but it's precisely through suffering that God chisels away at our imperfections to form us to be the complete and whole person He designed us to be. James 1:2–4 says, "Count it all joy, my brothers, when you meet trials of various kinds, for you know that the testing of your faith produces steadfastness. And let steadfastness have its full effect, that you may be perfect [*teleios*] and complete, lacking in nothing."

James isn't telling us to put on a façade and ignore our pain. He was no stranger to trials, and neither were his readers. He was the brother of Jesus, which meant he saw the deep suffering Jesus endured, and eventually James himself was killed for his faith.[10] In his letter, James is reminding us that we truly rejoice because trials will form in us a spiritual maturity ("perfect and complete") that is strengthened as we remain under the weight of our suffering. George Guthrie wrote in his commentary on James: "As a diamond is formed in the grip of extreme pressure, so the valuable character trait of endurance is crafted in the crucible of trials."[11]

To be clear, there are some trials from which God gives us a way of escape. We don't need to stay in an abusive relationship, avoid getting help for illnesses, or endlessly punish ourselves as some sort of penance for our failures. James isn't talking about staying in situations where God has provided a way out. That'd be like staying in a burning building when we should be sprinting to safety. And if He hasn't yet provided a way out, we can still ask Him. Even Jesus did that when He prayed, "Father, if you are willing, remove this cup from me" (Luke 22:42). Surrender, though, requires us to trust God with His response to that prayer, not ourselves.

As long as we live in this fallen world, we will experience suffering. So instead of frantically attempting to outrun it, let's learn to suffer well. Instead of endlessly chasing fleeting comfort and ease, let's stand firm. Because when we faithfully endure whatever it is God has called us to endure, that faithfulness will have the effect of making us truly, deeply, biblically perfect.[12]

As Jesus said in the Sermon on the Mount, we have a heavenly Father who is perfect. It's His perfection that enables us to remain steadfast in our struggles and surrender all we have to Him. Every attribute of God, He is in its entirety. He is that trait completely, and He cannot improve upon it. He can never be *more* loving, *more* just, *more* of any of His attributes. He is wholly, fully all that He is, and when we know and believe that to be true, we can let go of our need for ultimate control over our work, our parenting, our families, our goals, our possessions, and open our hands to receive whatever God wants to give us. We can submit all we are and all we have to Him for kingdom use. We can follow Him wherever He leads, resting in His perfection and knowing He is making us perfect along the way.

GRACE FOR WHAT LIFE IS

In 2014, my cousin Ryan was diagnosed with primary progressive multiple sclerosis. This neurological disease forced Ryan, his wife, Stacy, and their three kids onto a terrifying roller coaster they never wanted to ride. They've been thrown ICU visits, a feeding tube, bouts of pneumonia, rehab, appointments with specialists, and more. So much has been stripped away from their lives, and in the middle of it all after a particular harrowing season in March of 2022, Stacy wrote this:

> I hung up the phone after a work meeting about an annual report. My colleagues knew I was on my way to buy our new house and the excitement was palpable. Thirty minutes later I jumped in the van with my mother-in-law, and we left to get Ryan from respite care so we could head to the closing.
>
> I walked into Ryan's room. His eyes were closed and his mouth was hanging open. I touched his arm and his skin felt

hot. I lost my mind. I yelled. I grabbed a thermometer because I always have one with Ryan. He had a fever. I tried to get him to talk, look at me, or communicate with me in any way.

Within minutes EMTs were in his room, and one of them looked at Ryan and immediately said to me, "Does he have a pulse?" We should have been on our way to buy our new house and instead an EMT asked me if my husband had a pulse. Forty-five minutes later he was in the emergency room on a ventilator.

As I wrote in my first update a month ago, He's a God of the hills and valleys, and we experienced that firsthand this past month. Instead of going to buy a new home, Ryan fought another round of pneumonia. Instead of enjoying his new bedroom, he was in the hospital. Instead of drinking coffee, he got all his hydration and nutrition via feeding tube for the past month. Instead of celebrating with us at this miracle house, Ryan didn't see us for days as he worked with his rehab team to grow stronger.

This past month certainly didn't go as planned . . . far from it . . . but we've learned to grieve what we wish life was and soak up grace for what life is.[13]

Letting go of perfectionism means grieving what we wish life was and soaking up grace for what life is. It's in this kind of surrender—this giving up of what we expect or want or think we've earned and giving in to what God wants—that He makes us perfect. We won't reach that perfection in this life, but we can be sure no work of God will be left undone. He will one day finish what He has started in us.

The suffering you're dealing with is not for nothing. He's doing a work in you that cannot be accomplished through your own earning, your own striving, your own perfectionism. He's doing a work that requires surrender and endurance . . . the often slow plod of putting one foot faithfully in front of the other. But we can be assured that He will form in us something far greater than we could ever accomplish on our own. And He will give us the grace we need to get there.

REFLECT

1. In what ways do you struggle with perfectionism? How do you treat others who don't live up to your perfectionistic expectations?

   When certain things don't meet our expectations or slip out of our control, the way we respond can reveal the perfectionism in our heart.

2. Jesus called the rich young ruler to let go of his wealth because it was holding him back from being a fully devoted follower of Christ. If you were in the young man's position, what would Jesus be asking you to surrender?

3. What hard circumstances are you facing right now? What does it look like for you to be steadfast and endure, allowing God to form you to be mature and complete?

   Meditate on Paul's encouragement from 1 Thessalonians 5:23–24: "Now may the God of peace himself sanctify you completely, and may your whole spirit and soul and body be kept blameless at the coming of our Lord Jesus Christ. He who calls you is faithful; he will surely do it."

Chapter 9

INSIGNIFICANCE

Your Labor Is Not in Vain

Therefore, my beloved brothers, be steadfast, immovable, always abounding in the work of the Lord, knowing that in the Lord your labor is not in vain.

- 1 Corinthians 15:58

It is the ordinary that groans with the unutterable weight of glory.

- Robert Farrar Capon

A FEW YEARS AFTER I became a mom, a friend asked me, "What has surprised you most about motherhood?" My answer wasn't the messiness or sleeplessness or feeling like I didn't know what I was doing. Those things overwhelmed me, but everyone told me I would fight tiredness and feelings of inadequacy as a mom. I knew they would be a part of life with little ones.

"It is way more boring than I expected," I replied without much thought. My words startled me. I was busy all the time. I had a never-ending list of tasks and little arms constantly gripping my shirt, needing something from me. Even so, I couldn't help but feel bored by the tedium.

Maybe that's terrible to admit, but especially during the toddler to preschool years, I've struggled with the monotony of my days. I wholeheartedly love my kids, and those years bring a particular brand of hilarity and joy. But the season of molding Play-Doh into snakes and reading books with three words on each page and following around tiny humans who can barely walk without injuring themselves has not been my favorite. And I think the root of my boredom during that time stemmed more from a seeming lack of purpose than merely not enjoying toddler-aged activities.

> **What a discouraging reality it would be if the significance of life could only be found in its highlights.**

I like to feel productive, like I'm making a difference. I want my work to matter. And I know motherhood matters; of course it does. But when we break the big picture down into the nitty-gritty details of life, it can be hard to remember our work makes a difference. Raising my kids matters, but does cutting grapes in half matter? Does vacuuming the kitchen floor only to have it covered in pasta noodles five minutes later matter? Why continue to do our everyday tasks when they all too quickly get undone or when we don't see tangible progress?

Even if we aren't parents, we all have days when we wonder if our mundane work has any real significance. Maybe we experience a highlight here and there, but they are the exception. What do we do about everything in between? We're just sitting in another meeting, paying another bill, making another appointment. We're writing, creating, tending, helping, and working in whatever role God has set in front of us, and sometimes we can't help but wonder: *What's the point?*

What a discouraging reality it would be if the significance of life could only be found in its highlights.

When we don't see results from our work or our work gets undone or we're not sure if our vocation is even important in the first place, our everyday lives can feel insignificant. But the significance of our lives and work doesn't hinge on the flashiness of our highlight reel. It doesn't have anything to do with our achievements or how many people notice our work.

Our work is significant because God uses our ordinary faithfulness, nothing can be wasted on Jesus, and the new creation life has already started.

THE SIGNIFICANCE OF ORDINARY FAITHFULNESS

During the time of the judges, Israel was in a season of unrest. They seemed to live in a cycle of disobedience, judgment, rescue, and then disobedience all over again. A famine came over the land, and a man named Elimilech, his wife, Naomi, and their two sons traveled to the land of Moab. Elimilech died, the two sons married Moabite women—and then the sons died. Now, in the midst of famine in a land not her own, Naomi is a widow with two widowed daughters-in-law, Orpah and Ruth. The women are in vulnerable positions, unable to support themselves with no economic or social status.[1]

Naomi hears there may be food back in Israel, so she heads home and urges her daughters-in-law to return to their mother's house. Maybe there, they can prepare to remarry and start a new family.[2] Orpah agrees, but Ruth clings to Naomi, pleading to stay with her.

The two women travel back to Bethlehem: Naomi returning to the land she knew well; Ruth arriving as a foreigner. She had grown up in enemy territory, worshiping other gods. But she's given up her own people and sworn to care for Naomi even through death. One commentator explains that "Ruth's decision to be buried in Naomi's land would show that she was totally setting aside her former allegiances and dependencies to cast her lot in with Naomi."[3] Ruth is all in. She's fully committed to Naomi, and therefore fully committed to Israel and Israel's God.

The women need food, so Ruth gathers grain in the field of a man named Boaz, a well-respected relative of Naomi. Boaz provides for Ruth, and she ends up boldly asking him to marry her. He agrees, thus inheriting the cost of providing for both Naomi and Ruth and any children who would come after.

We don't know Ruth's name because of her résumé. Hers is not a story retold for generations because of the degrees she obtained or the number of people she impacted while she was alive. She doesn't speak to crowds. She doesn't write bestselling books. She doesn't earn millions. She doesn't have social status. She doesn't perform miracles. She doesn't prophesy or teach or do any work we often deem significant or meaningful. What does she do, instead?

> Our work doesn't have significance because we did it, but because of what God does with it.

Ruth picks up barley from the ground. She supports her mother-in-law. She figures out a way to survive. She takes one step of faithfulness after another in her very ordinary—and very hard—life. According to the world's standards, this poor widow from a rival nation didn't accomplish much at sll.

This story is one of unwavering commitment. It's about steadfast love and faithfulness shown between Ruth, Naomi, and Boaz. But the greatest significance comes at the very end of the book when the narrator wrote: "Now these are the generations of Perez: Perez fathered Hezron, Hezron fathered Ram, Ram fathered Amminadab, Amminadab fathered Nahshon, Nahshon fathered Salmon, Salmon fathered Boaz,

Boaz fathered Obed, Obed fathered Jesse, and Jesse fathered David" (Ruth 4:18–22).

Ruth's story is not about what she did but about what God did through her. It's about how He used her steadfast love and faithfulness to preserve the entire people of Israel and make way for the One who would save the world. The last few verses of the book of Ruth trace her genealogy through King David, the most famous and honored king of Israel. We can easily gloss over that list of names, but let's not miss the weight of what's written in these final few verses. Scholar Daniel Block explained:

> This book and this genealogy demonstrate that in the dark days of the judges the chosen line is preserved not by heroic exploits by deliverers or kings but by the good hand of God, who rewards good people with a fulness [sic] beyond all imagination. These characters could not know what long-range fruit their compassionate and loyal conduct toward each other would bear. But the narrator knows. With this genealogy he declares the faithfulness of God in preserving the family that would bear the royal seed in troubled times and in rewarding the genuine godliness of his people.[4]

Our work doesn't have significance because we did it, but because of what God does with it. The first chapter of Matthew traces Ruth's descendants all the way through to Jesus. Look at the providence of God in watching over Ruth, who wasn't even an Israelite, and guiding her to take ordinary, faithful steps to bring about the birth of the Son of God!

Ruth couldn't have known she would be the great-grandmother of King David. Even the narrator of her story would have had no idea her steadfast commitment would one day lead to the birth of the Messiah. Yet this is so often what God does. This is how He works. He doesn't need our grand acts or our lists of achievements. He doesn't need anything from us at all. Instead, He wants to use our faithfulness.

We're not given the backstory, but I wonder if it was a mother who packed five loaves and two fish for the boy who offered them to Jesus (John 6:9). I wonder if the boy had a mom who sighed to herself, tired of making his lunches each day. Did she feel unimportant or overlooked? Did the boy come running back home to her, breathlessly shouting about how a teacher named Jesus made that meal feed thousands?

I think of Timothy's grandmother Lois and his mother Eunice, two women mentioned briefly by Paul, not because of their accomplishments, but because of their faithfulness. When Timothy was young and these women taught him the truth about God, did they ever wonder if their efforts would make a real difference (see 2 Tim. 1:5 and 3:15)?

And the story of Job—he had everything. The house, the kids, the reputation, the money. Still, it wasn't those things that God used to work in his life and impact believers for thousands of years afterward. It was his faithfulness—even after he sat alone in the town dump, scraping his sores with the shards of a pot.[5]

God is not impressed by what we bring or limited by what we can't. Everything we have is from Him in the first place. What matters in the kingdom is not our status or abilities, but whether we've been faithful with what we've been given.

Faithfulness means there's something we're banking on that we cannot see. There's a result to come that we can't quite get our hands on yet. We're willing to play the long game instead of looking for instant gratification. And when we trust God to use whatever we have for the kingdom, the burden of insignificance falls away. We don't have to fear that our very ordinary lives are a waste because the apostle Paul wrote: God can do "far more abundantly than all we ask or think, according to the power at work within us" (Eph. 3:20).

HE IS WORTHY OF IT ALL

Watchman Nee, a Chinese church leader in the twentieth century, told a story of walking along a city street in his hometown in 1929, ragged and in poor health. He ran into an old professor, and the two men stopped at a tea shop to talk. The professor looked him up and down and said, "Now look here; during your college days we thought a good deal of you, and we had hopes that you would achieve something great. *Do you mean to tell me that this is what you are?*"[6] Watchman Nee had spent his life leading the church in China, and all this professor could see was a washed-up shell of a man who should have done so much more with his life. According to the professor, Nee had wasted his life.

"Waste," Nee wrote: "means, among other things, giving more than is necessary. . . . Waste means that you give something too much for something too little. If someone is receiving more than he is considered to be worth, then that is a waste."[7] Jesus, he points out, is never too little. He is worthy of *everything*.

When Mary, the sister of Martha, anointed Jesus with expensive perfume, Judas thought it was a waste, but not because he wanted to use the money from that ointment to serve others. For starters, Judas was a thief and took what he wanted from the moneybag. But he also did not understand the worthiness of Jesus. If he had, he would have known that no amount of ointment poured out on Jesus could ever be a waste (see John 12:1–8).

In his vision, the apostle John saw a sealed scroll that no one was worthy to open. He wept because of it. But one of the elders said, "Weep no more; behold, the Lion of the tribe of Judah, the Root of David, has conquered, so that he can open the scroll and its seven seals" (Rev. 5:5). John sees a Lamb who takes the scroll, and the living creatures and elders around sing, "Worthy are you to take the scroll and to open its seals, for you were slain, and by your blood you ransomed people for God from every tribe and language and people and nation, and you have made them a kingdom and priests to our God, and they shall reign on the earth" (vv. 9–10). Then thousands upon thousands of voices shouted around the throne. "Worthy is the Lamb who was slain, to receive power and wealth and wisdom and might and honor and glory and blessing!" (v. 12). In this chorus John witnesses in his vision, "Every created thing which is in heaven and on the earth and under the earth and on the sea is giving glory to God and to the Lamb."[8] If we think Jesus is unworthy of whatever we have to offer, then we do not know the real Jesus.

The death of Christ, His victory over sin and death, His resurrection, and His forever rule and reign make Jesus worthy of *everything*. If that is true, then nothing we do for the glory of God in the name of Jesus through the power of the Holy Spirit is a waste. Paul told the Colossian church, "Whatever you do, in word or deed, do everything in the name of the Lord Jesus, giving thanks to God the Father through him" (Col. 3:17). None of it is insignificant. None of it goes unnoticed by our Savior who is worthy of it all.

LIVING AS A NEW CREATION

For many years, I wrote online about food. I blogged about recipes, took photos, and shared dishes I enjoyed. At the same time, I worked for a hunger-relief organization. I remember thinking, *Is this okay?* I felt a very real dissonance between my hobby and my day job. I wasn't sure whether it was even appropriate to spend my days creating in my kitchen and savoring new dishes when the rest of the week I talked about severe hunger and malnutrition around the world. What value did creativity have in a world that's starving?

Before I threw in the towel and gave up on my creative work, I started to dig into what Scripture said about beauty, art, and specifically, food. I was once again reminded of how God tells His people throughout His Word to feed those who are hungry and care for those who are in need. I also began to see more clearly how God gave us food not just for sustenance, but also for delight. He gave us meals as a way to remember what He's done. He provided grains, grapes, and olives so that we could enjoy and create even more beauty with what He's given (see Ps. 104:14–15). Even the way we eat and drink can be done for the glory of God and the good of His kingdom.

When Jesus rose from the dead, it was the very meeting of heaven and earth. His resurrection was the beginning of a new creation, a new way of living and working in a new kingdom. Therefore, those of us who have been raised with Christ are called to live a different way. We "put on the new self, which is being renewed in knowledge after the image of its creator" (Col. 3:10). How we live now is meant to reflect who God is and the new creation that will one day come in its fullness. "If anyone is in Christ," Paul says, "he is a new creation. The old has passed away; behold, the new has come" (2 Cor. 5:17).

Here and now, we live as new creation people in a broken and hurting world. That means we create beauty because the new creation ruled by Christ is beautiful. We work for justice because God is perfectly just. We feed the hungry because we have been invited to the marriage supper of the Lamb with the Lamb of God. What we do now is a foretaste of what's to come—and that gives our work deep, lasting significance.

N. T. Wright said it this way:

> But what we can and must do in the present, if we are obedient to the gospel, if we are following Jesus, and if we are indwelt, energized, and directed by the Spirit, is to build *for* the kingdom. This brings us back to 1 Corinthians 15:58 once more: what you do in the Lord *is not in vain*. You are not oiling the wheels of a machine that's about to roll over a cliff. You are not restoring a great painting that's shortly going to be thrown on the fire. You are not planting roses in a garden that's about to be dug up for a building site. You are—strange though it may seem, almost as hard to believe as the resurrection itself—

accomplishing something that will become in due course part of God's new world.[9]

Sometimes our work can feel insignificant because we have an anemic view of the resurrection. The resurrection is about raising us to eternal life with Christ, absolutely. But it is also about God establishing a new kingdom on earth as it is in heaven. He is doing a new thing (Isa. 43:19), and in His grace, He invites us to participate in that work.

Our acts of service, creation of beauty, works of justice, words of teaching, care for creation, everything aligning with who God is and what His kingdom is about is not for nothing. All our work done through the power of the Spirit to honor God and serve our neighbor, build up the church, and bring glory to God is all part of living out our resurrection life here on earth.

Paul takes a whole section of his letter to the Corinthians to explain that the resurrection is real and has drastic implications for how we live *now*. Then, 1 Corinthians 15 ends with him saying, "Therefore, my beloved brothers, be steadfast, immovable, always abounding in the work of the Lord, knowing that in the Lord your labor is not in vain" (v. 58). If the resurrection is true, we have good and holy and sacred and exciting and sometimes even very ordinary work to do.

The work of the Lord unquestionably includes the overt and essential practices of teaching God's Word, telling others about the gospel, and all the "spiritual" activities many of us readily associate with living a Christian life. But it *also* includes everything else the Spirit calls us to do in order to reflect the kingdom and the character of God.

Musician and author Andrew Peterson talks about the difference between work being "overtly Christian" or "deeply Christian."[10] We need both. We need the bold and unashamed preaching of God's Word. We also need our art, our music, our child-rearing, our attitudes at work, our gardening, our everyday faithfulness to be a reflection of a deeply Christian way of living.

As Peterson wrote:

It is our duty to reclaim the sacredness of our lives, of life itself. And the first step is to remember—to remember the dream of Eden that shimmers at the edges of things, . . . to remember that work and play and suffering and celebration are all sentences in a good story being told by God, a story arcing its way to a new creation.[11]

OUR HIDDEN LIVES

The film *A Hidden Life* tells the story of an Austrian farmer, Franz Jägerstätter, who was executed by the Nazis in 1943.[12] Jägerstätter, a devoted Catholic, refused to fight for the Nazis or align himself with Hitler in any way. The beauty of the film, in my opinion, is in the ordinariness of life it displays. Much of the film shows Franz and his wife, Fanni, working their land, raising animals, and refusing to give into the daily pressure of the townspeople who could not understand why this couple would betray their nation.

Toward the end, after suffering and grief, after being disowned and enduring all kinds of physical toil, Fanni says a line I won't soon forget. The movie shows her going about her daily tasks without her husband, sweating and dirty and worn. She works the field, tends to the sheep, and slices apples at a table. With a soft and surrendered voice, she says, "The time will come when we will know what all this is for. And there will be no mysteries. We will know . . . why we live."[13]

I breathed deeply when I heard her words. Belief like Fanni's frees us from the lie of futility and infuses our work with meaning. The pouring out of our lives, the daily trying to live as a new creation person, words of kindness, unseen acts of service, the creation of beauty—there is purpose in all of it.

The movie finishes with a quote from George Eliot, a nineteenth-century English novelist. She wrote, "For the growing good of the world is partly dependent on unhistoric acts; and that things are not so ill with you and me as they might have been, is half owing to the number who lived faithfully a hidden life, and rest in unvisited tombs."[14]

The work of those standing on public platforms matters. But so do the hidden lives of people walking an unglamorous, ordinary, and even painful road of faithfulness.

REFLECT

1. What parts of your ordinary life do you struggle to find purpose in? What tasks leave you asking, "What's the point?"

2. Consider the story of Mary pouring perfume on Jesus' feet (see John 12:1–8). Who do you identify with in that story? What do you think your response would have been to Mary's actions?

3. Your labor in the Lord is not in vain. How does knowing that truth change the way you go about your work and life? What would you do differently if you fully believed that your work for the kingdom will last for eternity?

Chapter 10

DESPAIR

Waiting for God to Work

I believe that I shall look upon the goodness of the LORD in the land of the living! Wait for the LORD; be strong, and let your heart take courage; wait for the LORD!

> * PSALM 27:13–14

Christians, at their best, are the fools who dare believe in God's power to call dead things to life.

> * ESAU MCCAULLEY

MY BROTHER KNOCKED on my bedroom door at our childhood home. "It's happening," he said. I jumped out of bed, threw on a sweatshirt, and ran downstairs to my parents' room. All my siblings and I had moved away from home years before. But that week, we'd returned to the house with the cedar siding and floral wallpaper, not for a holiday or a celebration, but to be there when Mom died.

We had known this day was coming. About seven months earlier, the oncologist said she didn't think my mom would make it until

Christmas. But here we were on a February morning, weeping and listening to those final guttural breaths the hospice nurse warned us about.

Cancer had devoured my mother's body. Her skin hung over her bones and the smile she held on to as long as she could had faded. She was ready. And I was ready for her to not be in pain, for her to not have to deal with bed sores and fight to put air in her lungs and consume a whole pharmacy's worth of medication just to take the edge off.

After she died, my dad, sister, and I removed her soiled clothes and dressed her in the clean outfit she'd picked out a few weeks before. I'd helped take care of her for months, but these few minutes caring for her limp frame undid me. I didn't expect her to feel so heavy when alive, she had been skin and bones, almost no weight at all. I remember crying as we laid her back on the hospital bed and set her hands gently on her stomach. All there was to do now was wait for her body to be picked up.

Eventually, two men arrived to take her away. But they came earlier than we had anticipated, so we asked for more time. *Can you come back later? Don't take her quite yet. Please.* They understood, and kindly returned after a few hours, wrapped her in a black bag, and carried her out the front door. Just like that, she was gone.

I remember that moment as if it were yesterday. I remember feeling, as Leif Enger wrote in *Peace Like a River*, "a grief so hard I could actually hear it inside, scraping at the lining of my stomach, an audible ache, dredging with hooks as rivers are dredged when someone's been missing too long."[1] That scraping hurt like nothing else I'd ever experienced. God denied our prayers; He said no to our pleas for her health. Along with her body, the hope of healing left in a black bag out our front door.

WHEN IT'S TOO HARD TO HOPE

Sometimes, our hopes feel like milk bottles stacked in a pyramid shape in a carnival game. Life is the baseball, aimed, thrown, and knocking down each hope one by one. We hope the treatment will work. *Smack!* We hope our marriage will heal. *Smack!* We hope our finances will turn around. *Smack!* We hope justice will be served. *Smack!* Life hits those hopes hard, and down they crash. It's all too tempting to give up, believe nothing is going to change, and sink into despair.

Despair says hope has run dry. Despair looks at our circumstances and declares, "Why bother trying? Just give up." Despair is the phrase spoken by Job's wife when she said, "Curse God and die" (Job 2:9). Even for those of us who have grown up hearing the Christian message of hope, despair still lurks around the corner, waiting to pounce when hope feels weak. Grief forces you to ask if your hope is real and if it's worth holding on to.

I knew my mom loved Jesus, and I believed God would one day raise her body back to life. But watching her be carried out in that bag through the door caused me to reckon with the truth of my hope in a way I'd never had to do before. *That* body will come back to life? *Seriously, God?*

When we look at our circumstances, despair can seem far more in line with reality than hope. Hoping a dead body will one day walk around healed and restored and glorified . . . that truth doesn't align with what my eyes saw that morning. Holding on to the hope that justice will one day roll down like waters doesn't make sense when we watch people get away with corruption and abuse and all kinds of evil. Hoping God will remake a world coming apart at every seam—that kind of hope feels foolish. Where is God? Why bother holding on to Him when He leaves us with all (waving my hands wildly) *this*?

WAITING ON GOD

We're not the only ones who have been tempted to despair. The Old Testament prophet Habakkuk grieved the wickedness and injustice he saw in Israel, and he was angry God didn't seem to be doing anything about it. "O LORD, how long shall I cry for help and you will not hear? Or cry to you 'Violence!' and you will not save? Why do you make me see iniquity, and why do you idly look at wrong?" (Hab. 1:2–3a). *When are You going to finally show up, God?* God answers that He's doing something about it—He's *been* working. And part of His plan includes using the nation of Babylon to bring justice.

This response seems to set Habakkuk over the edge. Babylon is more wicked than God's people! How could a good God answer this way? After all, the law said, "A land on which blood was shed could not be purified through sacrifice but only by shedding the blood of the murderer (Num. 35:33). Thus, a city or society built by bloodshed and oppression cannot endure."[2] The prophet appeals to God's character, saying, "You who are of purer eyes than to see evil and cannot look at wrong, why do you idly look at traitors and remain silent when the wicked swallows up the man more righteous than he?" (Hab. 1:13). What's happening in the world doesn't jive with what Habakkuk thought he knew about God.

God makes it clear He will deal with all wickedness and save His people in the process (Hab. 3:13). He answers Habakkuk, but God doesn't resolve all the questions. In the meantime, the prophet can only wait. "I will take my stand at my watchpost and station myself on the tower, and look out to see what he will say to me, and what I will answer concerning my complaint" (Hab. 2:1).

We don't like waiting. We like our instant pots and our high-speed internet and our same-day delivery. We want our emails answered within minutes and our children to "just hurry up and get in the car." Most of us are woefully bad at waiting—and waiting on God is no exception. "Whether in prayer or prophecy, contemporary worshipers demand that God act according to the dizzying schedule of those pressed for time," wrote one commentator.[3] Then if God doesn't act on our schedule, we pull a move like Abram did when he slept with Hagar in an attempt to fulfill God's promise a little faster. *He's taking too long, we think. We'd better just go ahead and figure it out on our own.*

But God has never been pressed for time. He's never been in a rush or scrambling to get out the door. He's never looked at His watch and realized He missed an appointment or was late making good on a promise. No. The sovereign God works in ways we can't always understand and on a timetable we don't usually like.

After a tumultuous history of being slaves, fleeing Egypt, wandering in the wilderness, and finally coming into the land God promised to them, Joshua 21:45 says, "Not one word of all the good promises that the LORD had made to the house of Israel had failed; all came to pass."

Think of how much frustration the Israelites would have saved themselves if they believed that truth *before* God's promise was fulfilled. When the spies scoped out the land of Canaan, all but Joshua and Caleb returned saying it would be too hard and the people in the land were too powerful to overcome. Instead of believing God, "All the congregation raised a loud cry, and the people wept that night. And all the people of Israel grumbled against Moses and Aaron" (Num. 14:1–2a). But rather than boiling in their angst, they could have rested in the certain and secure hope that God's promises would never fail.

Habakkuk's posture is far different from that of Israel back in Numbers. His example reveals that our suffering doesn't have to lead us to despair. It can lead us to a place of trust, joy, and security while we wait on God to do what He said He'll do.

It's in this waiting that the prophet finally says the words most familiar in his book:

Though the fig tree should not blossom,
nor fruit be on the vines,
the produce of the olive fail
and the fields yield no food,

the flock be cut off from the fold
  and there be no herd in the stalls,
yet I will rejoice in the LORD;
  I will take joy in the God of my salvation.
GOD, the Lord, is my strength;
  he makes my feet like the deer's;
  he makes me tread on my high places. (Hab. 3:17–19)

Habakkuk's words hinge on the reality that he knows God will make good on His promises. Until the darkness becomes light and tears turn to joy, the prophet watches and waits, trusting that God will come through in the end.

COMPLAIN IN GOD'S DIRECTION

It's all too easy for us to wonder what God is doing and why He won't do it faster. It's tempting to walk away from God angry and bitter like the Israelites. Or, like Abram, we try to fix our problems without God. We let our questions and our doubts lead us away from God, when instead they are the very things He often uses to lead us toward Him.

We cannot fight despair by pretending everything's okay or denying the reality of our pain. Sometimes we expect hope to act as a mere bandage for our wounds or a tissue to wipe away the tears. Maybe we believe hope means we (or others) should "get over it" a little faster or perk up and force a smile. It's true and beautiful that we don't weep as if we have no hope (1 Thess. 4:13). But it's also true, as Tish Harrison Warren put it, that hope doesn't diminish our weeping.[4] Instead, we can cry every last tear. True hope

> **Despair says that there's no point in coming to God at all, but hope complains in God's direction.**

140

says we can face every grief head on. We can lament and mourn, and God hears it all.

Like David, we can ask, "How long, O Lord? Will you forget me forever?" (Ps. 13:1). With Job we can admit, "I loathe my life. . . . Does it seem good to you to oppress, to despise the work of your hands and favor the designs of the wicked?" (Job 10:1, 3). Even Elijah went so far as to say, "I have had enough! Lord, take my life" (1 Kings 19:4 csb).

Waylon Bailey wrote in his commentary on Habakkuk:

> Human nature tends to be filled with complaints, but human beings typically complain in the wrong directions. . . . We tend to talk about God rather than talk to him; we tend to complain about God rather than complaining to him. Habakkuk took his complaints directly to God.[5]

Despair says that there's no point in coming to God at all, but hope complains in God's direction. Hope recognizes this is not the way things are supposed to be and begs God to do something about it. I don't think we can come to a place of true hope like Habakkuk without getting on our knees and doing some serious wrestling with our Maker. And when we do, even if questions and struggles remain, we'll see we have a God who hears the cries of His people, a God still at work in the world— even when His methods and timing don't make sense to us.

Through lament, through honest cries before our God, we can finally come to a place that admits, "the only thing to do is to hold the spectacular promises in one hand and the messy reality in the other and praise YHWH anyway."[6]

HE KNOWS OUR GRIEF

While my mom was sick, I read *The Magician's Nephew* by C. S. Lewis.[7] The book is set as the prequel to *The Lion, the Witch and the Wardrobe*, and Digory, the main character, is a young boy whose mother is sick. I felt Digory's grief in my own heart and grappled with many of the same questions he asks. My mom, just like Digory's, lay in bed in the next room, her health continuing to fail while I desperately prayed for healing.

As the story goes, Digory eventually meets Aslan, the lion, who prepares to send him on a mission in Narnia. Aslan asks Digory if he's ready, and Digory considers for a moment that he might make a deal with the lion: *I'll help you if you help Mother.* But he thinks better of bargaining with Aslan and replies with a simple, "Yes."

Tears start to form in Digory's eyes because it seems like the hope for his mother's healing is fading away. He can't stop the words pouring out, "But please, please—won't you—can't you give me something that will cure Mother?"[8]

Digory lifts his eyes to look at Aslan's face—and what he sees surprises him more than anything. The lion isn't looking at him with pity or disdain. He isn't annoyed by the boy's plea. Instead, Aslan himself bends down toward Digory. His own eyes well with tears, and Digory can't help but wonder which of the two of them is sadder about Mother.

"'My son, my son,' said Aslan. 'I know. Grief is great.'"[9]

I pleaded with God countless times, "But please, *please*—won't you—can't you do something to heal my mom? *Please?*" I begged Him for healing, and I knew He could. Digory ended up receiving a magic apple that healed *his* mom. Why wouldn't God heal mine?

That's where many of us sit right now—in the in-between place of unknowns and questions and doubts where it feels like hope is lost. Maybe we're angry at God, ready to walk away from waiting for Him any longer. But it's here, in this seemingly hopeless middle, that God not only hears our cries and our laments, but He even goes so far as to lean in next to us while we weep in the darkness. He puts His arm around our shoulders, presses our head against His chest. And He waits with us for the morning.

Isaiah tells us that the Suffering Servant "was despised and rejected by men, a man of sorrows and acquainted with grief; and as one from whom men hide their faces he was despised and we esteemed him not" (Isa. 53:3). Jesus knew rejection, humiliation, and suffering. He was "'acquainted with grief'—literally, 'known by grief,' as a man is known by a friend."[10] There is no sorrow He doesn't know, no pain He hasn't Himself endured. It was this very Savior hanging on a cross who cried out in anguish, "My God, my God, why have you forsaken me?" (Matt. 27:46).

So often we despair because we feel alone in our pain. No one understands us, and no one gets what we're going through. Maybe it sounds like a Christian cliché to respond, "Well, Jesus gets it." But that truth can only become a cliché if we've sugarcoated the pain of our Savior. We can only dismiss the truth that He understands when we've dismissed *His* suffering.

God incarnate started His life in the womb of a poor, humble teenager. He suffered through a sham trial, died a horrific death, and was buried in a borrowed tomb. The Son of God—though there was no deceit in His mouth, no sin in His heart, no words wrongly uttered—endured suffering of the worst kind. *He gets it.*

He knows your grief.

THE ROAD TO EMMAUS

Luke tells the story of two disciples walking from Jerusalem to Emmaus, a journey of about seven miles.[11] Their teacher, Jesus, was a prophet they had once thought was the Messiah who would save Israel. But this Jesus had just been mocked and flogged. He'd been murdered, put to death for crimes He didn't commit. The two companions carried searing pain from the deepest sorrow on their faces thinking Jesus must not have been the One.

The disciples are possibly heading home after celebrating Passover in Jerusalem, but the events of the weekend have been anything but festive. They hang their heads and kick a few rocks down the dusty path in frustration. Silence punctuates their anxious conversation. They don't know what to make of all that's happened. They're confused by the rumors about Jesus' body being gone. They're not sure if they should believe the testimony of some of the women who supposedly encountered angels at Jesus' tomb. *There's no way that could be true,* they may have thought. Besides, they don't know of anyone who has actually seen Jesus alive (Luke 24:24).

Yet even deeper than their confusion sits a layer of sadness. It was grief, yes—but messier. They grieve the loss of their Teacher. But more than that, they grieve the loss of their hope. There's no such thing as a dead Messiah.

Another man joins in the conversation as they walk along the road. He asks them, *What are you both talking about?* "And they stopped walking and looked discouraged" (Luke 24:17 CSB).

I imagine them staring at their feet, trying to hide tears—maybe even a dose of anger—from this stranger. Maybe they shake their heads at Him in disbelief. I wonder how much time passes before Cleopas speaks up. *Where in the world have you been? he says. How could anyone not know what's been going on the last few days?! Didn't you hear what happened to Jesus?* "But we had hoped that he was the one to redeem Israel. Yes, and besides all this, it is now the third day since these things happened" (v. 21).

We had hoped. But apparently, hope is lost. We even, for a moment, believed those claims about rising from the dead or something else crazy happening on the third day. It's the third day, and . . . nothing. We're still under Roman rule. Our Teacher, the prophet who did all those miracles and healings, is dead. And now, no one can even find His body.

The man who joined these two on the road, the one who appears clueless about what's going on in the world, continues speaking. He starts with Moses and traces the biblical story through the Prophets and into the present. *Don't you get it?* He asks.

The three arrive in Emmaus, and the two disciples beg this newfound friend to stay with them and eat a meal. It's late, after all, and everyone's tired. So, this stranger-turned-friend takes them up on their offer of hospitality, and as they're about to eat, this man breaks bread, blesses it, and passes it out. There's a strange familiarity to His movements, the way He took on the role of host even though He was a guest, the way He prayed and then broke the bread. *Why does it feel like we've already lived this moment?* They can't help but think about the Teacher they just lost, the times He took bread, blessed it, broke it, and passed it out— especially that one time they were with a crowd of five thousand and the baskets of bread mysteriously never emptied.

And they can hardly believe their eyes. *Jesus!*

Then Jesus disappears. *What in the actual world?* The two disciples are floored. Maybe they stand stunned for a second, but their bodies can't stay still much longer. They shovel a few bites of that very blessed bread into their mouths and run out the door those seven miles back to Jerusalem.

They find where the Eleven have gathered, along with a few others. I picture Cleopas and his companion bursting through a door, but before the words escape their mouths, the Eleven and others exclaim, "The Lord has risen indeed, and has appeared to Simon!" (v. 34). Then the two disciples, still out of breath, hands on their knees from their unexpected 10k-plus run from Emmaus, feverishly relay their own story. *He's alive! We just saw Him too!*

They tell about meeting Jesus on the road and how their hearts burned inside them and how they finally recognized Him when He broke bread

Then Jesus shows up. "Peace to you!" He says. I picture Him grinning, excited to share the joy of His resurrection. Maybe He even chuckles at the fact that He scared the living daylights out of His friends.

At first, those gathered fear Jesus is a spirit. Even though Simon, Cleopas, and another disciple have seen the risen Christ, a sliver of doubt wedges its way into the souls of many there. But Jesus shows them His hands and feet, they see the nail marks and touch His body. *We can hardly believe it! It's really Him.*

All the fear, discouragement, grief, heartache, and loss turns to joy. The room fills with shouts and hugs and tears of joyful disbelief (Luke 24:41).

These men and women, this group of Jesus followers, have survived tragedy and oppression. They've suffered profound disappointment and witnessed murder and injustice. They've tasted their fair share of grief and will no doubt take in more in the years to come. But here they see firsthand that hope, as it turns out, has not been lost. Hope is standing right in front of them.

HE WHO PROMISED IS FAITHFUL

Maybe, once upon a time, you hoped. You hoped God would heal, change, restore. But you're staring at the very real and very hard life in front of you, and it seems the hope you once had has all been swept away. So now, you're left walking from one day to the next, sure that the events of the past have secured the death of your future. You're left choosing between despair and hope, and doesn't despair come a little more naturally sometimes?

But as a line from *Every Moment Holy* says, "It is only false hopes that are brittle."[12] Our hope is sure and steadfast—not because we always are, but because God always is. So don't give up. Don't stop waiting on God. Don't stop asking Him your questions and bringing Him your doubts. Don't stop complaining in His direction. He can take it! The God who made the universe also sits with us in our grief, and the God who sits with us in our grief is also the One who overcame it through the resurrection.

We have hope, not just for this life but for the one to come. Because Christ has died, Christ is risen, and Christ will come again. So, "Let us hold fast the confession of our hope without wavering, for he who promised is faithful" (Heb. 10:23).

REFLECT

1. When have you felt like you lost hope?

2. Pastor and author Mark Vroegop wrote, "When I'm stuck between my tears and what I believe, lament is the language I need."[13] Are you stuck between your tears and your belief? Practice lament this week. If you're not sure how to start, pray through psalms of lament, such as Psalms 13, 42, or 73.

3. Take a few minutes to meditate on the reality of the resurrection. You may want to consider reading through 1 Corinthians 15. Do you believe Jesus rose from the dead, that His body came back as a new and glorious version of Himself? It's a crazy notion, but it changes everything.

Chapter 11

WHAT TO CARRY INSTEAD

Let us also lay aside every weight, and sin which clings so closely,
and let us run with endurance the race that is set before us,
looking to Jesus, the founder and perfecter of our faith, who for the
joy that was set before him endured the cross, despising the shame,
and is seated at the right hand of the throne of God.

     • HEBREWS 12:1–2

Whether I live another day or many decades more, there is only
one way all of this will end, and that is with me in your arms,
O Father, joyful and utterly whole, pressing even further for all
eternity into your beauty, wisdom, love, and delight.

     • DOUGLAS KAINE MCKELVEY

IN J. R. R. TOLKIEN'S *The Return of the King*, the third book in The Lord of the Rings trilogy, Frodo has been carrying the infamous ring on an impossibly long journey. He and his ever-devoted friend, Sam, are nearing the end of their quest, and they eventually collapse in exhaustion and fall asleep. When Sam awakes, he tries to rouse Frodo, but Frodo can only manage a few grunts and groans. They've been traveling so far for so long; but here, at the end, he can't muster another step.

Sam looks at Frodo, considering what to do next. With determination and unshakable devotion, he heaves Frodo onto his back as he says, "Come, Mr. Frodo! . . . I can't carry [the ring] for you, but I can carry you and it as well. So up you get! Come on, Mr. Frodo dear! Sam will give you a ride. Just tell him where to go, and he'll go."[1]

Thank the Lord for people like Sam who pick us up when we can't keep going. And the truth is that we all have something—or someone— to carry. Like Frodo had to carry the ring, and Sam had to carry Frodo, there are responsibilities and roles God calls us to take on our back. But we're equipped to carry those things because we've been freed from all the other burdens like worthlessness or insecurity or despair. We're equipped because Jesus Himself carries our burdens with us.

CARRYING OUR CROSS

In Matthew 16, Jesus tells His followers to take up their cross and follow Him. It's a statement that can get lost on our modern ears, but to the disciples, the Teacher's words would have been appalling. Craig Keener explained the gruesomeness of carrying one's cross:

> Carrying the horizontal crossbeam en route to crucifixion . . .
> often meant enduring mockery and scorn on a path leading
> to death as a condemned criminal. Crucifixion was the worst
> form of criminal death, the supreme Roman penalty, normally
> inflicted only on lower class provincials and slaves; even talk of it
> could evoke horror.[2]

We can't soften Jesus' words by rushing to make His call metaphorical. Theologian R. T. France noted in his commentary that Jesus quite literally calls His disciples to risk everything, to follow Him through persecution and suffering and death, which many of them eventually did.[3] But it wasn't long after Jesus' call that they all ran away and deserted Him as He faced His own death.

We've so often done the same. We've chosen self-preservation over bold belief, comfort over crucifixion. Our decisions make sense when the here and now is all we see. But "faith is the assurance of things hoped for, the conviction of things not seen" (Heb. 11:1). Do we believe that the "things not seen" will be worth our steadfast endurance now?

Jesus' words can sound like He's asking us to haul a load that will kill us—and it might. It did for many of the disciples, anyway.

> **Self-preservation now only gives us what *this* life has to offer. But following Jesus—even to death—gives us *everything*.**

But before we groan with the anticipated weight of just one more thing, let's remember Jesus doesn't ask us to carry anything He hasn't carried Himself, and the Holy Spirit fuels us with the strength to take each step.

There's no resurrection without a death—and there's no true life without dying to self. Jesus asked His listeners, "For what will it profit a man if he gains the whole world and forfeits his soul?" (Matt. 16:26). The heaviest of burdens is the one that causes you to lose your soul.

Self-preservation now only gives us what *this* life has to offer. But following Jesus—even to death—gives us *everything*. Peter wrote to a persecuted church:

> According to his great mercy, he has caused us to be born again
> to a living hope through the resurrection of Jesus Christ from

the dead, to an inheritance that is imperishable, undefiled, and unfading, kept in heaven for you. . . . Though you do not now see him you believe in him and rejoice with joy that is inexpressible and filled with glory. (1 Peter 1:3–4, 8)

There cannot be a better inheritance, a more worthwhile reward, than what God Himself gives His children.

CARRYING EACH OTHER'S BURDENS

I hope none of us faces the type of persecution Jesus and His disciples did. Our modern lives look far different than theirs. But whatever hardships or grief or trials we have in this life, Jesus doesn't ask us to shoulder our load alone. He is with us always, to the end—and all the while we are led by the very Spirit of God (see Matt. 28:20 and Rom. 8:14).

He's also given us each other. In Galatians 5, after reminding His listeners that we have freedom in Christ, Paul says we're to use that freedom to serve. Our freedom from our burdens is the very thing that enables us to help bear the burdens of others.

Galatians 6:2 says, "Bear one another's burdens, and so fulfill the law of Christ." In the context of the passage, Paul specifically tasks the church through spiritual restoration (v. 2) and financial support (v. 6). We cultivate a community where we can come alongside those battling sin and admit to ourselves where we've gone wrong. And through our finances, we can help bear the burden of those tasked with teaching the Word.[4]

But Paul's call, no doubt, extends even beyond what he directly references. We can help others practically, spiritually, and emotionally. We can bring meals to a family with a sick loved one, we can listen without judgment and without inserting our opinions, we can mourn with those who mourn, we can encourage one another, and we can meet material needs.

Six months before my mom died, family gathered at a beach house for a final family vacation.[5] This trip wasn't one any of us really wanted to take—or at least under these circumstances. It'd be the last time we'd all be together while my mom was still alive.

One evening, we brushed remnants of sand off our feet and shuffled into the family room of the rental house. My parents, siblings, and our spouses squeezed onto the worn couches, while a few nieces and nephews sat on the floor. My mom sat next to my dad, and the two of them updated us on her cancer prognosis. Mom's T-shirt sagged, and every once in a while, her eyes closed mid-conversation.

We talked about what hospice would look like, their financial picture, and when my dad would take a leave of absence from work. We asked if he could adequately care for her in the wake of his own cancer diagnosis a year earlier. It's a conversation I wish I'd never had to have, but I'm grateful for it. Not many people get to ask such blunt questions and be given honest answers.

I stared at the carpet, shifting my weight in my seat every few minutes and mentally cursing the old sofa for my discomfort. We passed around a box of tissues. You could hear the sound of sniffles and see reddened eyes. I tried to listen and be present, but I could think only about the gaping hole in my own future.

My mom would never be there when I had kids. She'd never be in the hospital with me as I labored or come visit and let me take a nap. Before that, she'd never go to Target to help me register or throw me a baby shower. My kids would never call out, "Nana!" and she'd never answer the phone when I needed advice on potty training or picky eating.

I felt silly and stupid mourning a reality that was years away. She was in front of me, dying of cancer, and my mind fixated on losses that hadn't even happened yet. But somehow the weight of the future grief felt almost heavier than the present. At one point, I mumbled those feelings out loud, and my mom turned her head to look me in the eyes. Even without words, I understood she was grieving the same loss.

Grief doesn't live only in the moment. It steals a piece of the future—one you wonder about, long for, and miss—even though you never really had it.

My sister-in-law spoke up. "I know it's not the same thing," she confessed. "I know there's nothing like having your mom with you, and I know there's no replacement for her. But we're going to be there."

A decade later, I can attest how that promise has been kept far beyond what I expected. Family and friends have stocked my freezer with meals, watched my kids when I needed a break, checked in during hard seasons, listened while I cried. Grief still catches me off guard sometimes, but I've known the relief that comes when others help carry that load.

In 2 Corinthians 7:5–7, Paul mentions that Titus was a great encouragement to Paul and his companions. He wrote:

> For even when we came into Macedonia, our bodies had no rest, but we were afflicted at every turn—fighting without and fear within. But God, who comforts the downcast, comforted us by the coming of Titus, and not only by his coming but also by the comfort with which he was comforted by you, as he told us of your longing, your mourning, your zeal for me, so that I rejoiced still more.

Paul confessed his body had no rest. Yet just a couple sentences later, he wrote of how he rejoiced. What happened in the middle? *Being comforted by God through other believers.* As the people of God led by the Spirit of God, this is what we are called to do—to love one another by carrying each other's burdens, just as Christ carried our burdens to the cross.

When we carry each other's

> **The ways we love one another are seeds we put in the ground that God will not let die.**

burdens, we help bring joy out of weariness. The strain of physical tiredness may remain, but joy can be there too. I experienced that with my family after my mom died. The heartache of losing her will never disappear, but new joy has grown alongside it.

Toward the end of his letter to the Galatians, Paul wrote, "And let us not grow weary of doing good, for in due season we will reap, if we do not give up" (Gal. 6:9). The ways we love one another are seeds we put in the ground that God will not let die. He takes what we offer through the Spirit and multiplies it far beyond what we can fathom. I think one day, we'll be surprised by what sprouts up from those seeds. God will show us not that our acts were all that grand but that He can do a whole lot with very little. Or like one author said, "For we will discover that what we reap is completely out of proportion to what we've sown."[6]

Friend, we have work to do. We have a cross to carry and others' burdens to help bear. But this kind of calling is one that gives us the very life we most deeply desire. Coming to Jesus and carrying the yoke He offers means we get to do things His way with His help. And His yoke will not crush us. It will not leave us lonely or purposeless or fearful, like other kinds of burdens do. Taking up what He offers gives us the truest, deepest rest, because it leads us right into the arms of our Savior. Thanks be to God.

REFLECT

1. What does it look like for you this week to carry your cross, to follow Jesus with *everything*?

2. Whose burdens can you help carry? Do you need to ask someone to help carry yours?

3. What burdens from the rest of this book do you struggle with most deeply? Go back to that chapter and find some of the Scripture passages used. Choose one or two to meditate on this week.

Appendix

INTERVIEW WITH A THERAPIST

As I mentioned in the beginning of All Who Are Weary, *my words are one tool among many that God can use to help us find the deep rest our souls need. Counseling is another tool, and I invited writer and therapist Melissa Brownback to share a few insights from her perspective as a licensed professional clinical counselor.*

1. What are some of the distinctives separating professional counseling from other types of counseling? What are some of the types of counseling or therapy?

PROFESSIONAL COUNSELING IS a state-regulated industry designed to uphold training, clinical standards, and accountability for practitioners as well as protection for consumers in the event of malpractice. In order to obtain a license as a professional counselor, one must (1) obtain a masters or doctoral degree in clinical psychology, mental health counseling, or a related field, (2) pass both national and state required examinations, (3) complete approximately 3,000 hours (minimum of two years) of practice under a licensed supervisor, and (4) complete continuing education courses to maintain licensure. Professional counselors hold the following credentials (titles may differ from state to state): Licensed Professional Clinical Counselor, Licensed Professional Counselor, Licensed Clinical Social Worker, Licensed Marriage and Family Therapist, and Licensed Psychologist.

Pastoral counseling and other forms of lay counseling are provided within the context of the local church or parachurch organizations. This format of counseling is typically best suited for short-term care and crisis management, or when an individual desires a deeper understanding of what the Bible has to say about their particular issue. There are also several lay counseling organizations that offer training and certification for volunteers to walk alongside those who are hurting in their church communities. While pastoral and lay counseling offers help to many people, it is important to note that pastors and lay counselors often do not have the appropriate training nor professional regulation to treat complex issues like trauma, severe depression and anxiety, panic attacks, and suicidal ideation.

Most professional counselors use an eclectic blend of different counseling theories and interventions. Professional counselors who identify as Christian counselors may also integrate biblical/theological concepts into their counseling practice alongside their chosen therapeutic modality. The most common approaches to counseling are:

- Cognitive-Behavioral Therapy: focuses upon understanding the beliefs you hold about yourself and engaging in thought and behavioral experiments to challenge patterns of thought, feelings, and behavior that aren't working for your life and relationships.
- Psychodynamic Therapy: examines your attachment style and relationships with primary caregivers to better understand the

places where you find yourself stuck or repeating old patterns in your current life and relationships.

- Narrative Therapy: utilizes storytelling to better understand the themes of your particular story and provides clients with the opportunity to actively live a new story in their present life and relationships.
- Trauma Therapy: utilizes body-centered approaches to assist clients in reprocessing and reintegrating traumatic memories/experiences.

2. In the book, I talk about letting go of the burden of worry, but what is the difference between worry and the kind of anxiety that may require therapy, medication, etc.?

Worry and anxiety are universal to the human experience. While anyone could experience benefits from processing their worry or anxiety with a counselor, people who experience more severe forms of anxiety often require the help of trained professionals in order to obtain relief from their symptoms.

If you or a loved one are experiencing any of the following, I would consider your experience of anxiety to fall within the moderate to severe range, and I would highly recommend seeking out the help of a professional counselor in your area:

- Excessive, daily anxiety or worry for over three months
- A significant increase in anxiety/worry following a major life transition (e.g., a move, having a baby, starting a new job, ending a significant relationship)
- Panic attacks (e.g., hyperventilation, excessive heart rate, chest pain, nausea)
- Inability to leave one's home without severe anxiety or panic attacks
- Flashbacks and/or nightmares of a traumatic event

In some cases, your therapist might recommend scheduling an evaluation with a psychiatrist to assess if medication would be helpful for you. Antidepressant medications have been shown to have efficacy in the treatment of anxiety and are commonly prescribed to treat it. In some cases, anti-anxiety medications are prescribed for the short-term management of severe panic attacks and anxiety. However, these medications are classified as a controlled substance due to their addictive properties and should be used with caution and under the supervision of a medical professional.

3. What is clinical depression, and how is it different from common feelings of sadness or discouragement?

Similar to our discussion about anxiety in the previous question, feelings of sadness and discouragement are common to everyone, usually subside within a few days, and don't cause significant disruption to our lives and relationships. However, there are a few distinguishing factors which differentiate a typical bad mood from clinical depression, which we often refer to as a "depressive episode."

The primary symptoms of depression include (1) depressed mood and/or (2) loss of interest or pleasure in all, or nearly all activities for a minimum of two consecutive weeks. Significant weight loss/gain, insomnia/hypersomnia, and feelings of worthlessness or guilt are also very common when an individual is experiencing depression.

In my practice, I see experiences of depression in the following categories:

• Grief: deep sadness following the death of a loved one.
• Mood Dysregulation: this is what people most often think of when they hear the term "clinical depression." These clients experience what is known as a "depressive episode," which is characterized by low mood, feelings of worthlessness and/or disproportionate guilt,

loss of interest in things one previously enjoyed, sleep disturbances, fatigue, difficulty concentrating, and recurrent thoughts of death. These episodes may be singular or cyclical in nature.

- Stress and Trauma: oftentimes, the root of a client's depressive symptoms lies in response to stressful life circumstances (e.g., job loss, having a baby, moving, end of a significant relationship) or trauma.

4. Do you have any advice for someone who may be realizing they may need help from a therapist? Where do they start? What are some questions they can ask to find someone who can help them best? Are there any pros and cons from getting help from various types of therapists or counselors?

For anyone who is questioning whether they may need to see a professional counselor, I would tell them that there is never a bad time to reach out to a therapist! Sometimes, it can be even more helpful in the long run to reach out for help before we reach the point of crisis or burnout due to living in extreme survival mode.

When it comes to finding a professional counselor, my top recommendation is to find someone who truly feels like a good fit for you, even if it means trying out a few different therapists. I will never forget what one of my graduate school professors told our class the very first day of my counseling program: "The most important predictor of success in the counseling relationship is the connection between the counselor and the client." Now that I have been in practice for over a decade, I have experienced this statement to be true over and over.

One of the best ways to find a great therapist is to reach out to the people you trust for a personal recommendation. Sometimes knowing that one of our people trust and feel safe with a person is helpful in developing a solid relationship with a counselor. (*The only caveat to this would be if you want to work on a relationship issue with that trusted person. In that case, it's usually best practice to not see the same therapist.)

Another great place to start is to ask your church if they have a referral list of professional counselors in your area. Church referral lists typically contain therapists who have been vetted by staff and have a reputation of being responsive and helpful.

And finally, if the first two resources are not available to you, you can search professional databases like Psychology Today or your insurance network.

Most professional counselors offer free 10- to 15-minute phone consultations prior to scheduling a first appointment. While it may be scary to talk to someone you've never met on the phone, I highly recommend taking advantage of this! Consultations are great for getting a feel for a therapist's style and personality.

Here are a few questions you can ask:

- What is your approach to counseling/therapy? (See Question 1 for an overview of different therapeutic approaches.)
- How do you integrate your faith into the counseling process?
- What is your experience working with [insert your specific issue]?
- Do you have any specialty areas?

In certain cases, professional counselors may recommend a consultation with a psychiatrist if they determine you may benefit from adding medication to your treatment. My personal approach is to recommend medication if I notice a client has reached a level where daily functioning is excessively impeded due to severe depression and/or anxiety symptoms (e.g., unable to get out of bed, unable to work or care for children, unable to complete daily tasks without panic attacks).

5. Can you offer any advice for someone who is trying to support someone else struggling with anxiety, depression, or other mental illness? How can we help carry those burdens, especially if we ourselves have never struggled with them in the same way?

I love this question! While I am so thankful for helping professionals, we all need a support system in our lives. Here are a few practical ways that you could support a person struggling with their mental health:

Listen without Fixing

While it may seem counterintuitive, people who are experiencing depression and/or anxiety are not looking for answers and advice from the people in their lives. What they do need is a supportive presence who will listen with compassion and without judgment. If you're looking for some go-to phrases to help support a loved one, you can start with these:

"That sounds so hard/heavy."
"I'm here for you."
"You are loved/worthy/valuable."

Learn Alongside Them

Oftentimes in therapy, counselors will provide book or podcast recommendations as a part of the healing process. If you have a close friend or spouse who is reading/listening to something their therapist recommended, offer to read/listen with them (as long as the subject matter feels doable for you). You could even schedule a coffee date to talk through what you're learning together.

Offer Practical Support

It can be so painful to watch our loved ones suffer through seasons of depression and/or anxiety and not be able to take those feelings away.

However, one of the things we *can* do is offer help in practical ways. Here are a few ideas:

- Write an encouraging, handwritten note
- Drop off a favorite coffee, tea, or small bouquet of flowers
- Offer to babysit
- Bring over a meal or grocery items
- Schedule time to go for a walk together

6. When we are trying to support a friend or loved one, how do we know when we've taken on too much? Maybe we simply don't have it to give, or they need someone with professional training to address more deep-seated issues.

When it comes to walking alongside a friend or loved one who is struggling, I would recommend regularly checking in with yourself for signs of burnout. If you find yourself consistently exhausted by the relationship, anxious or frustrated when your friend or loved one texts or calls, panicky about their physical safety, or if you've lost the capacity to feel empathy and compassion for them and the problems they're facing, it's time to refer that person to a professional. I would especially never recommend being the sole source of support for someone wrestling with suicidal ideation, substance abuse, or severe trauma.

Melissa Brownback is a licensed therapist, writer, and founder of Thrive Counseling Collective. She has over ten years of experience walking alongside individuals, couples, and families in their journeys of healing and growth. Melissa specializes in working with women, survivors of abuse and trauma, attachment, and couples in crisis. She is a SoCal transplant with Midwestern roots, pastor's wife, and mom of two amazing boys. You can connect with her on Instagram (@melissabrownback) or on her website www.melissabrownback.com.

ACKNOWLEDGMENTS

TO MY AGENT, Dan, and to Trillia, Catherine, Amanda, and the whole team at Moody—your encouragement, wisdom, and feedback has been invaluable. Thank you for seeing something worthwhile in my words and making this book far better than I could have on my own.

To my fellow writers I also get to call friends: Ann Swindell and the WWG Mastermind crew; the Coffee + Crumbs team and Exhale community; Michelle Reyes, and my fellow Redbud writers—creativity is so much better when done in community, especially when that community includes beautiful and thoughtful people like you.

Melissa Brownback, it seems like yesterday we were chatting in that café in Waco. Thank you for sharing your wisdom as a therapist and all-around incredible human.

Sonya, Katie, Ashlee, where do I even start? You've been midwives to this book, *our* book. Friends for life.

To Steve and Sarah Erickson and Meadowland Church—I didn't know at the time that what I shared with you would become part of this bigger project. Thank you for letting me work out my words with you all.

Ryan and Stacy, it's an honor to tell a piece of your story. You've continually pointed to our faithful God as you live a life of faithfulness.

To so many people who have not only supported me in the writing of this book but who have walked alongside me as I lived these stories: my Redeemer family and the Batavia CG; and to Jennifer, Caeli, and Shae, who have cried with me during dark seasons, celebrated the joyous ones, and been willing to read my early drafts. I will always be grateful for our friendship.

To Jane—the "truth versus lies" homework you gave me years ago was the first seed of this book. God has used you to bring me through some dark seasons, and thank you hardly suffices. But *thank you.*

Dad, your fingerprints are all over these pages, and you've shown me what living out true rest looks like. Carol, Grady and Lora Sue, and my whole family, thank you for your continued encouragement and support in writing and in life. I'm forever grateful. Mom, I miss you every day. But I know now in a way I didn't know before that the resurrection is real.

To Eric and Krista—this book wouldn't have happened without you. Krista, at that beach house you told me you'd be there for me after Mom died. You've done more than I could have ever imagined. Also, it seems I haven't come that far from writing papers at your kitchen table while eating your leftover pancakes.

Jenn and Paul, you've let me invade your home with a vanload of kids more times than I can count. And I will never take for granted the luxury of writing in a soundproof room.

Samuel, Josiah, Elijah, and Isabel, I love you a googol times infinity. I'm finally done writing my book. Let's go get some ice cream.

And to Colson—I'm Frodo on the side of the mountain. And you've picked me up and carried me, time and time again. I love you.

NOTES

INTRODUCTION

1. Corrie Ten Boom, *The Hiding Place* (New York: Bantam Books, 1971), 195.

CHAPTER 1: FINDING REST FOR YOUR SOUL

Epigraph: Saint Augustine, *Confessions*, trans. R. S. Pine-Coffin (New York: Penguin Books, 1961), 132.

1. Portions of this section were adapted from an article written for (in)courage: "A Truth to Combat the Lies," November 21, 2019, www.incourage.me/2019/11/a-truth-to-combat-the-lies.html.

2. Portions of this section were adapted from an article written for Risen Motherhood: "Finding Rest for Our Souls: Letting Go of Our Burdens and Taking Up What Christ Offers Instead," August 30, 2021, www.risenmotherhood.com/blog/finding-rest-for-our-souls-letting-go-of-our-burdens-and-taking-up-what-christ-offers-instead.

3. Craig Blomberg, *Matthew*, vol. 22, The New American Commentary (Nashville: B&H Publishing Group, 1992), 193.

4. Craig S. Keener, *The IVP Bible Background Commentary: New Testament* (Downers Grove, IL: IVP Academic, 2014), 75.

5. Keener, *The IVP Bible Background Commentary: New Testament*, 75.

6. C. S. Lewis, *Letters of C. S. Lewis: Edited and with a Memoir by W. H. Lewis*, ed. Walter Hooper (New York: Houghton Mifflin Harcourt, 1966), 285.

7. David Andersen, "Knowing the Best Is Yet to Come," CaringBridge, December 14, 2012, www.caringbridge.org/visit/charlotteandersen/journal/view/id/51be5db66ca004c3280034d8.

8. Quoted by Dallas Willard, *Life Without Lack: Living in the Fullness of Psalm 23* (Nashville: Thomas Nelson, 2018), xv.

CHAPTER 2: WORTHLESSNESS

Epigraph: Daniel Nayeri, *Everything Sad Is Untrue: A True Story* (New York: Levine Querido, 2020), 16.

1. A version of this story was adapted from an article written for The Joyful Life: "Finding Joy Through the Darkness," March 24, 2020, www.joyfullifemagazine. com/finding-joy-through-the-darkness/.

2. K. A. Mathews, *Genesis 1–11:26*, vol. 1A, The New American Commentary (Nashville: B&H Publishing Group, 1996), 175.

3. John H. Walton et al., *The IVP Bible Background Commentary: Old Testament* (Downers Grove, IL: IVP Academic, 2000), 29.

4. "In the ancient world an image was believed to carry the essence of that which it represented." (Walton et al., *The IVP Bible Background Commentary: Old Testament*, 29). For example, a carved idol was an image of a god, and that image was not simply an object you worshiped. The carved image or idol wasn't the god itself but carried the very "essence" of the god, and the god accomplished his work through the image. When Adam and Eve, then, are created in the image of God, the implication is that human beings, while not themselves God, are the ones God uses to accomplish His purposes on the earth.

5. Diane G. Chen, *Luke: A New Covenant Commentary* (Eugene, OR: Cascade Books, 2017), 109. While this woman's appearance at the dinner party was surprising, the ability to gain access to such a party was not abnormal. As Diane Chen says, "In ancient banquets the doors were left open so that people could come in and listen in on the intellectual exchanges around the table."

6. Diane Chen's commentary is helpful when trying to visualize this scene. She wrote, "Since diners recline around a U-shaped low table, leaning on their left side, with their feet stretched out behind them, the woman has access to Jesus' feet without disturbing the proceedings." See Chen, *Luke: A New Covenant Commentary*, 109.

7. Craig S. Keener, *The IVP Bible Background Commentary: New Testament* (Downers Grove, IL: IVP Academic, 2014), 199.

8. D. Martyn Lloyd-Jones, *Spiritual Depression: Its Causes and Cure* (Grand Rapids, MI: Eerdmans, 1965), 66.

CHAPTER 3: CONDEMNATION

Epigraph: Dane Ortlund, *Gentle and Lowly: The Heart of Christ for Sinners and Sufferers* (Wheaton, IL: Crossway, 2020), 194.

1. A version of this story first appeared on Coffee + Crumbs: "You Are Not a Failure," September 30, 2020, www.coffeeandcrumbs.net/blog/2020/9/30/you-are-not-a-failure.

2. Eugene Peterson, *A Long Obedience in the Same Direction: Discipleship in an Instant Society* (Downers Grove, IL: InterVarsity Press, 2000), 27.

3. See also Genesis 3:1–5 and Job 1:6–12.

4. Kenneth L. Barker, "Zechariah," in *The Expositor's Bible Commentary: Daniel-Malachi*, ed. Tremper Longman III and David E. Garland (Grand Rapids, MI: Zondervan, 2008), 723.

5. Barker, "Zechariah," 754. Also see Psalm 109:6.

6. Ibid., 755.

7. Ibid., 758.

8. John Bunyan, *The Pilgrim's Progress* (Minneapolis: Desiring God, 2014), 64.

9. Ramesh Khatry, "Revelation," in *South Asia Bible Commentary*, ed. Brian Wintle et al. (Grand Rapids, MI: Zondervan, 2015), 1790.

10. Athanasius of Alexandria, *On the Incarnation* (Blue Letter Bible, 2012), 16–17, Kindle edition.

11. Ibid., 21.

12. See Acts 8:1–3.

13. G. K. Beale, *Revelation: A Shorter Commentary* (Grand Rapids, MI: Eerdmans, 2015), 259.

CHAPTER 4: WORRY

Epigraph: Jackie Hill Perry, *Holier Than Thou: How God's Holiness Helps Us Trust Him* (Nashville: B&H Publishing Group, 2021), 145.

1. Johannes P. Louw and Eugene Albert Nida, *Greek-English Lexicon of the New Testament: Based on Semantic Domains* (New York: United Bible Societies, 1996), 312.

2. Louw and Nida, *Greek-English Lexicon of the New Testament: Based on Semantic Domains*, 312.

3. For the purposes of this chapter, the terms "anxiety" and "worry" are used interchangeably. But I am referring to the concept of worry that we all tend to struggle with. I am not attempting to address the issue of clinical, physiological *anxiety*.

4. Matthew 6:25–34.

5. Eugene Peterson, *A Long Obedience in the Same Direction: Discipleship in an Instant Society* (Downers Grove, IL: InterVarsity Press, 2000), 44.

6. Louw and Nida, *Greek-English Lexicon of the New Testament: Based on Semantic Domains*, 798.

7. Portions of this section were originally shared here: "When Cries of Distress Are All You Can Utter (Lament as Hope in Psalm 120)," April 17, 2020, www.sarahjhauser .com/blog/2020/4/17/when-cries-of-distress-are-all-you-can-utter-lament.

8. Dallas Willard, *Life Without Lack: Living in the Fullness of Psalm 23* (Nashville: Thomas Nelson, 2018), xxi.

9. Matthew 6:10.

10. Paul E. Miller, *A Praying Life: Connecting with God in a Distracting World* (Colorado Springs: NavPress, 2009), 125.

11. Tish Harrison Warren, *Prayer in the Night: For Those Who Work or Watch or Weep* (Downers Grove, IL: IVP Books, 2021), 57.

CHAPTER 5: SELF-SUFFICIENCY

Epigraph: Walter Brueggemann, *The Message of the Psalms: A Theological Commentary* (Minneapolis: Augsburg Publishing House, 1984), 49.

1. J. Alec Motyer, *The Prophecy of Isaiah: An Introduction & Commentary* (Downers Grove, IL: IVP Academic, 1993), 279.

2. A version of this story first appeared on Coffee + Crumbs: "You Don't Have to Do It All," October 25, 2019, www.coffeeandcrumbs.net/blog/2019/10/25/ you-dont-have-to-do-it-all.

3. N. T. Wright, *Surprised by Hope: Rethinking Heaven, the Resurrection, and the Mission of the Church* (New York: HarperCollins, 2008), 288.

4. Peter Wehner, "NIH Director: 'We're on an Exponential Curve,'" *Atlantic*, March 17, 2020, www.theatlantic.com/ideas/archive/2020/03/interview-francis-collins-nih/608221/.

CHAPTER 6: INSECURITY

Epigraph: Hannah Anderson, *All That's Good: Recovering the Lost Art of Discernment* (Chicago: Moody Publishers, 2018), 106.

1. Henri J. M. Nouwen, *Out of Solitude: Three Meditations on the Christian Life* (Notre Dame, IN: Ave Maria Press, 1974), 19–20.

2. Rupi Kaur (@rupikaur_), "We personalize what people think about us...," Instagram, May 4, 2022, www.instagram.com/p/CdJIvJ_lxr2/.

3. Sam Allberry, "Is God Anti-Gay?: A talk by Sam Allberry," *The Gospel Coalition Podcast*, podcast audio, April 11, 2019, https://podcasts.apple.com/us/podcast/ tgc-podcast/id270128470?i=1000434731725.

4. D. Martyn Lloyd-Jones, *Spiritual Depression: Its Causes and Cure* (Grand Rapids: Eerdmans, 1965), 34.

5. Timothy Keller, *The Freedom of Self-Forgetfulness: The Path to True Christian Joy* (England: 10Publishing, 2012), 39–42.

6. I'm indebted to Tim Keller for these insights about receiving compliments and criticism. See Keller, *The Freedom of Self-Forgetfulness*, chap. 2.

7. Alan Fadling, *An Unhurried Life: Following Jesus' Rhythms of Work and Rest* (Downers Grove, IL: InterVarsity Press, 2013), 53.

8. Henri J. M. Nouwen, *In the Name of Jesus: Reflections on Christian Leadership* (New York: The Crossroad Publishing Company, 1989), 27–28.

CHAPTER 7: COMPARISON

Epigraph: Timothy Keller, *The Freedom of Self-Forgetfulness: The Path to True Christian Joy* (England: 10Publishing, 2012), 35.

1. Alan Fadling, *An Unhurried Life: Following Jesus' Rhythms of Work and Rest* (Downers Grove, IL: InterVarsity Press, 2013), 16.

2. My own retelling of this story from Matthew utilizes the research of Kenneth E. Bailey that he shares in *Jesus Through Middle Eastern Eyes: Cultural Studies in the Gospels*. I've cited specific page numbers to show where I've more directly built on the foundation of his work.

3. Kenneth E. Bailey, *Jesus Through Middle Eastern Eyes: Cultural Studies in the Gospels* (Downers Grove, IL: InterVarsity Press, 2008), 357.

4. Ibid., 358–59.

5. Ibid., 360–61.

6. See Matthew 19:30 and Matthew 20:16.

7. Jackie Hill Perry, *Holier Than Thou: How God's Holiness Helps Us Trust Him* (Nashville: B&H Publishing Group, 2021), 119.

8. Craig Blomberg, *Matthew*, vol. 22, The New American Commentary (Nashville: B&H Publishing Group, 1992), 304. "Bad eye" is "a biblical image for stinginess and jealousy," wrote R. T. France. See R. T. France, *The Gospel of Matthew*, The New International Commentary on the New Testament (Grand Rapids, MI: Eerdmans, 2007), 751.

9. See Luke 18. Again here, throughout this retelling, I lean on Kenneth Bailey's research.

10. Craig S. Keener, *The IVP Bible Background Commentary: New Testament* (Downers Grove, IL: IVP Academic, 2014), 227.

11. Bailey, *Jesus Through Middle Eastern Eyes*, 348.

12. Ibid., 349.

13. Ibid., 348.

14. Luke 22:24–27.

CHAPTER 8: PERFECTIONISM

Epigraph: C. S. Lewis, *Mere Christianity* (New York: HarperOne, 2001), 205–206.

1. Matthew 5:19.

2. Jesus talked about six issues total when He gave examples of ways to show the "greater righteousness": anger, lust, divorce, oaths, retaliating, and loving enemies. See Matthew 5:17–48.

3. Johannes P. Louw and Eugene Albert Nida, *Greek-English Lexicon of the New Testament: Based on Semantic Domains* (New York: United Bible Societies, 1996), 745.

4. John R. W. Stott, *The Message of the Sermon on the Mount* (Downers Grove, IL: InterVarsity Press, 1978), 122.

5. Stott, *The Message of the Sermon on the Mount*, 124.

6. Craig Blomberg, *Matthew*, vol. 22, The New American Commentary (Nashville: B&H Publishing Group, 1992), 296.

7. R. T. France, *The Gospel of Matthew*, The New International Commentary on the New Testament (Grand Rapids, MI: Eerdmans, 2007), 734.

8. Ibid., 735.

9. N. T. Wright, *Surprised by Hope: Rethinking Heaven, the Resurrection, and the Mission of the Church* (New York: HarperOne, 2008), 286.

10. George H. Guthrie, "James," in *The Expositor's Bible Commentary: Hebrews–Revelation*, ed. Tremper Longman III and David E. Garland (Grand Rapids, MI: Zondervan, 2006), 199.

11. Guthrie, "James," in *The Expositor's Bible Commentary: Hebrews–Revelation*, 213.

12. A version of this section was originally shared here: "It Will Be Worth It (James Study Week 2, James 1:2–11)," August 17, 2020, www.sarahjhauser.com/blog/james-week-2.

13. Stacy May, "One Month," CaringBridge, March 16, 2022, www.caringbridge.org/visit/ryandmay/journal. Slightly edited for clarity.

CHAPTER 9: INSIGNIFICANCE

Epigraph: Robert Farrar Capon, *The Supper of the Lamb: A Culinary Reflection* (New York: Modern Library, 2002), 99.

1. John H. Walton et al., *The IVP Bible Background Commentary: Old Testament* (Downers Grove, IL: InterVarsity Press, 2000), 277.

2. Naomi encourages the women to go back to their *mother's* house, not their father's. The father is likely still alive (Ruth 2:11), but it was the mother who was the one to advise and prepare a daughter for marriage. "Therefore, Naomi's encouragement of the girls to return to their mother's home does not suggest seeking a place of legal protection, but rather a place that may provide a new family

situation." See Walton et al., *The IVP Bible Background Commentary: Old Testament*, 277.

3. Walton et al., *The IVP Bible Background Commentary: Old Testament*, 278.

4. Daniel I. Block, *Judges, Ruth*, vol. 6, The New American Commentary (Nashville: B&H, 1999), 736–37.

5. See Walton et al., *The IVP Bible Background Commentary: Old Testament*, 496. See also Job 2.

6. Watchman Nee, *The Normal Christian Life* (Carol Stream, IL: Tyndale House Publishers, 1977), 270.

7. Nee, *The Normal Christian Life*, 269.

8. G. K. Beale, *Revelation: A Shorter Commentary* (Grand Rapids, MI: Eerdmans, 2015), 118.

9. N. T. Wright, *Surprised by Hope: Rethinking Heaven, the Resurrection, and the Mission of the Church* (New York: HarperOne, 2008), 208.

10. Andrew Peterson, "Andrew Peterson: Christian Faith, the Arts and Imagination," C. S. Lewis Institute, YouTube, June 23, 2021, https://youtu.be/7PliT8KYNsw.

11. Andrew Peterson, "Every Moment Holy: New Liturgies for Daily Life," The Rabbit Room, November 3, 2017, www.rabbitroom.com/2017/11/every-moment-holy-new-liturgies-for-daily-life/.

12. I'm grateful to have been introduced to this film by Andrew Peterson when he was interviewed for the C. S. Lewis Institute: https://www.youtube.com/watch?v=7PliT8KYNsw.

13. *A Hidden Life*, directed by Terrence Malick (Fox Searchlight Pictures, 2019), 2:46:02, https://www.amazon.com/gp/video/detail/B083BLZN9N/.

14. This quote is from George Eliot's novel *Middlemarch*, quoted in *A Hidden Life*, directed by Terrence Malick, 2:48:38.

CHAPTER 10: DESPAIR

Epigraph: Esau McCaulley, "The Unsettling Power of Easter," *New York Times*, April 2, 2021, www.nytimes.com/2021/04/02/opinion/easter-celebration.html.

1. Leif Enger, *Peace Like a River* (New York: Atlantic Monthly Press, 2001), 54.

2. Kenneth L. Barker and Waylon Bailey, *Micah, Nahum, Habakkuk, Zephaniah*, vol. 20, The New American Commentary (Nashville: B&H Publishing Group, 1999), 337.

3. Ibid., 324.

4. Tish Harrison Warren, *Prayer in the Night: For Those Who Work or Watch or Weep* (Downers Grove, IL: InterVarsity Press, 2021), 50.

5. Barker and Bailey, *Micah, Nahum, Habakkuk, Zephaniah*, 293.

6. N. T. Wright, *Evil and the Justice of God* (Downers Grove, IL: InterVarsity Press, 2006), 60.

7. Parts of this story have been previously published here: "Digory's Plea, The Magician's Nephew + The Compassion of God," August 18, 2018, www.sarahjhauser .com/blog/2018/8/18/digorys-plea.

8. C. S. Lewis, *The Magician's Nephew* (New York: Scholastic Inc., 1983), 154.

9. Ibid.

10. Henri Blocher, *Songs of the Servant: Isaiah's Good News* (Vancouver: Regent College Publishing, 2005), 63.

11. Craig S. Keener, *The IVP Bible Background Commentary: New Testament* (Downers Grove, IL: IVP Academic, 2014), 243.

12. Douglas Kaine McKelvey, "A Liturgy for the Death of a Dream," in *Every Moment Holy* (Nashville: Rabbit Room Press, 2017), 234.

13. Mark Vroegop, "May His Cancer Heal Millions," *Desiring God*, January 8, 2019, www.desiringgod.org/articles/may-his-cancer-heal-millions.

CHAPTER 11: WHAT TO CARRY INSTEAD

Epigraph: Douglas Kaine McKelvey, "For Remembering How the Story Ends," in *Every Moment Holy: Volume II* (Nashville: Rabbit Room Press, 2021), 128.

1. J. R. R. Tolkien, *The Return of the King* (New York: Ballantine Books, 1966), 233.

2. Craig S. Keener, *The IVP Bible Background Commentary: New Testament* (Downers Grove, IL: IVP Academic, 2014), 87.

3. R. T. France, *The Gospel of Matthew*, The New International Commentary on the New Testament (Grand Rapids, MI: Eerdmans, 2007), 636.

4. In verse 3 of this passage, Paul says, "For if anyone thinks he is something, when he is nothing, he deceives himself. But let each one test his own work, and then his reason to boast will be in himself alone and not in his neighbor. For each will have to bear his own load." Paul is not contradicting himself here. The word translated "load" in the ESV is a different word than the one he uses for burden. It's used elsewhere to refer to the cargo of a ship or a knapsack. It refers more to the idea of personal responsibility. We are to carry each other's burdens, but we cannot ultimately rest on the spiritual laurels of others. We are accountable before God for ourselves. We are mutually responsible to one another as the church, but we are ultimately personally responsible for the choices we make and the way we use what God has given, the lives we live.

5. A portion of this story was shared at Coffee + Crumbs: "Picking Up the Pieces," June 25, 2019, www.coffeeandcrumbs.net/blog/2019/6/25/picking-up-the-pieces.

6. Todd Wilson, *Galatians: Gospel-Rooted Living*, ed. R. Kent Hughes, Preaching the Word (Wheaton, IL: Crossway, 2013), 218.

DO YOU FEEL TOO BUSY TO PRAY? THEN YOU'RE INVITED TO FIND REST IN GOD'S LOVING PRESENCE.

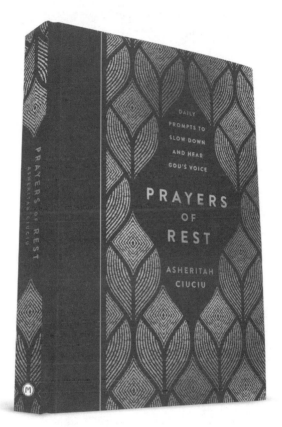